CW01669121

POOP AND LEARN

Useless Facts for your Time on the Throne

This book is intended for entertainment purposes. While all facts have been researched and verified to the best of our ability, this is not a textbook and no bathroom philosophers were harmed in the making of this book.

Welcome to the most productive bathroom break of your life!

This book is packed with useless knowledge you absolutely don't need but will definitely want. Whether you're here to impress strangers, win arguments, or just avoid scrolling your phone on the toilet again, you've come to the right place.

Inside, you'll find weird facts, forgotten stories, and strange trivia across topics like animals, food, the universe, the human body, history, and more. It's like a quiz night had a baby with your search history.

You can flip through at random or read cover to cover, but remember: you'll come out smarter than when you sat down. Probably.

Now sit down, relax, and prepare to get weirdly well-informed.

Willy Wiper

- Animals
- Food & Drink
- Pop Culture
- Science & Technology
- The Human Body
- Geography & The World
- The Universe
- History
- Sports & Games

Animals

Butterflies Taste With Their Feet

Butterflies don't use tongues to taste like we do. Instead, they have special sensors on their feet. When they land on a plant, they "taste" it to decide whether it's a good place to lay eggs. If it passes the taste test, the plant becomes a butterfly nursery.

Dolphins Call Each Other

Dolphins use unique whistles to identify one another, like names. Every dolphin develops its own signature sound, and others in the pod learn to recognize it. Scientists have even observed dolphins calling out a missing dolphin's "name" when it disappears. It's one of the clearest signs of complex communication in the animal kingdom and it shows how deeply social these creatures really are.

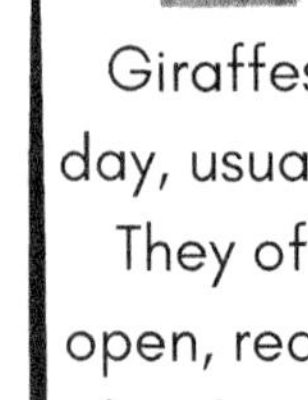

Giraffes Barely Sleep

Giraffes only sleep about 30 minutes to 2 hours a day, usually in short naps that last just a few minutes. They often sleep standing up, with their eyes half open, ready to run if danger approaches. Even when they lie down, it's usually just for a few minutes at a time. Their sleep schedule might sound exhausting to us, but it helps them avoid predators and survive in the wild.

Cows Have Best Friends

Researchers have found that cows form close friendships and become stressed when separated from their preferred companions. Their heart rates even drop when they're reunited. So the next time you see cows in a field standing side by side, it might not just be for shade. They might just be chilling with their BFF.

Sharks Have Built-In GPS

Sharks can sense the Earth's magnetic field, which helps them navigate like living compasses. This ability is so precise that some sharks have been recorded returning to the exact same beach they were born at, years later. No smartphone, no maps, just raw biological GPS.

Bees Recognize Human Faces

Despite their tiny brains, bees can remember and recognize human faces. Scientists taught bees to associate faces with sugary rewards and the bees learned to tell people apart. So if you swat at a bee today, don't be surprised if it gives you the side-eye tomorrow.

Sloths Are Good Swimmers

Even though sloths are famous for being slow, they're actually excellent swimmers. They use their long arms to paddle through water three times faster than they move on land. In the wild, they sometimes drop straight from a tree into a river below, which is probably the most energetic thing they do all week.

Elephants Comfort Each Other

When an elephant notices a friend in distress, it might wrap its trunk around the other or gently touch its face. They've even been seen standing quietly together until the upset elephant calms down. Scientists say this shows emotional intelligence, something elephants have in common with humans and very few other animals.

Parrots Name Their Babies

Wild parrots use unique sounds to identify each chick, almost like giving them names. These special calls stay with the parrots for life and help family members recognize each other. So yes, parrots were giving out personal names long before humans invented baby name books.

Ants Build Living Bridges

When ants need to cross a gap, they sometimes link their bodies together to form a living bridge. Other ants then walk across their backs. These insect bridges can change shape and size depending on what's needed and the ants rotate positions so no one gets too tired. It's teamwork at its finest: no talking, no meetings, just pure instinct and cooperation.

Hummingbirds Weigh Less Than Pennies

Most hummingbirds weigh between 2 and 4 grams. That's less than a single U.S. penny. Despite their tiny size, they have incredible energy. Their wings beat up to 80 times per second, and their hearts can race at over 1,200 beats per minute. To keep going, they eat constantly, visiting hundreds of flowers each day. Basically, they're tiny flying machines powered by sugar.

Octopuses Use Tools

Octopuses have been observed collecting coconut shells and empty shells to use as hiding places or shields. This kind of tool use is rare in the animal kingdom and shows just how clever these creatures are. Some even unscrew jar lids or solve mazes in lab tests. With flexible bodies and powerful brains, octopuses are among the most mysterious and intelligent animals in the ocean.

Frogs Can Freeze Themselves

Some frogs in cold climates survive winter by literally freezing. Their hearts stop beating, their blood stops flowing and their bodies become solid ice. But when spring arrives, they thaw out and hop away as if nothing happened. These frogs produce natural antifreeze-like substances that protect their cells from damage during the frozen months.

Ravens Are Great Problem-Solvers

Ravens have shown intelligence on the same level as young children. In tests, they've used tools, solved puzzles and even planned for the future. One study showed that ravens could figure out how to pull up a string to get food, even though the setup required several steps. They also remember who treated them kindly (and who didn't). Not bad for a bird often mistaken for a Halloween prop.

Koalas Have Fingerprints

Koalas have fingerprints that are nearly identical to those of humans. In fact, even under a microscope, it's hard to tell them apart. This has actually caused confusion at crime scenes in Australia, where koala prints have accidentally been mixed in with human ones. So if a cookie goes missing and there's eucalyptus breath in the air, you might want to question the local wildlife.

Turtles Can Breathe Through Butts

Some turtles have a special ability called cloacal respiration, which allows them to absorb oxygen through their behinds. This comes in handy during winter hibernation, when they're underwater for long periods. While it might sound like a party trick gone wrong, it's actually a clever survival tactic and one more reason turtles deserve our respect.

Wombats Poop Cubes

Wombats are the only animals known to produce cube-shaped poop. Their intestines contract in a slow, uneven rhythm that forms flat edges instead of round ones. This helps the poop stay put when marking territory, which is important in the wild. Scientists studied it for years and still agree that it's weirdly impressive.

Sea Otters Hold Hands

To avoid drifting apart while sleeping on the water, sea otters often float side by side and hold hands. They also wrap themselves in kelp to stay anchored. This adorable behavior isn't just cute, it helps them stay safe from predators and currents. Some even believe the hand-holding strengthens family bonds. Either way, it's one of the most wholesome habits in the animal world.

Camels Don't Store Water

Despite the myth, camels don't actually store water in their humps. The humps are made of fat, which helps them survive long periods without food. Camels stay hydrated because their bodies are incredibly efficient. They can lose up to 25% of their body weight through sweating without getting dehydrated. Their blood cells are also oval-shaped, which helps them keep circulation going even when water is scarce.

Pigeons Can Do Math

Pigeons might not look like geniuses, but studies have shown they can understand basic arithmetic. In lab tests, pigeons were able to compare numbers and even count objects in order. They've also been trained to distinguish between different styles of art and recognize themselves in mirrors. So next time you call someone "bird-brained," remember that some birds might actually be smarter than we think.

Bats Share Snacks

Vampire bats have a surprising social side: if one bat fails to find a blood meal, another will often regurgitate some of its own dinner to help. They remember who helped them in the past and return the favor later. It's a kind of blood-based trust system that scientists compare to friendships. Even among creatures with spooky reputations, kindness shows up in unexpected ways.

Zebras Confuse Predators

Zebra stripes don't just look cool. They help protect them from predators. When a herd of zebras runs together, the black-and-white patterns create a kind of optical illusion that makes it hard for lions to single out one target. Some researchers also believe the stripes help with temperature control or keep biting insects away. Stylish and smart.

Snails Take Long Naps

Some snails can sleep for up to three years at a time, especially in harsh conditions like droughts. During this long rest, their bodies slow down almost completely. Once the environment improves, they simply wake up and carry on. It's one of nature's strangest ways to deal with tough times. When in doubt, take a years-long nap.

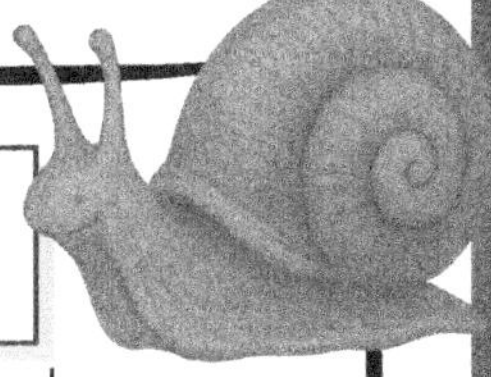

Dogs Understand Human Words

Dogs don't just respond to tone or body language. Studies using brain scans have shown that they can actually recognize specific words and distinguish them from nonsense sounds. Some dogs can learn over 100 words, and a few gifted ones even more. So yes, when you say "walk," your dog probably knows exactly what you mean and is already excited about it.

Chameleons And Camouflage

Many people think chameleons change color to blend into their surroundings, but that's not their main reason. They usually shift colors to regulate body temperature or communicate with other chameleons. For example, a brighter color can signal anger or excitement. So while their talents are still impressive, the truth is a little less spy-movie and a bit more mood ring.

Orcas Have Local Dialects

Orca whales live in family groups called pods and each pod has its own set of vocal sounds, like a local accent or dialect. These unique calls help orcas recognize their group members. Young orcas learn their pod's sounds by mimicking adults, just like human babies learn to speak. It's another sign of how socially complex and intelligent these animals really are.

Woodpeckers Have Shock Absorbers

A woodpecker can peck a tree over 20 times per second without hurting its brain. That's because its skull has special features that absorb the impact, including spongy bone and a flexible tongue that wraps around its head inside the skull. These adaptations protect the bird's brain and make it one of the toughest little headbangers in the animal kingdom.

Caterpillars Melt Into Butterflies

When a caterpillar turns into a butterfly, it doesn't just grow wings. Inside the cocoon, it completely dissolves into a soup-like substance. Its body breaks down into basic cells and from that liquid, the butterfly is built. Some parts of the caterpillar, like eye cells, survive and are reused. It's less like remodeling and more like starting from scratch.

Pandas Eat All Day

Giant pandas spend up to 14 hours a day eating bamboo. Despite being bears, their diet is almost entirely vegetarian and they need to consume a lot to get enough nutrients. They can eat over 10 kilograms of bamboo daily. Most of their day is spent chewing, napping and then chewing some more. It's a very slow and peaceful lifestyle.

Penguins Can Jump High

Even though they waddle on land, penguins are surprisingly powerful in the water. To launch themselves back onto the ice, they build up speed underwater and use tiny bubbles to reduce drag. Some species can jump more than 1.5 meters straight out of the water. It's like having built-in rocket boots powered by fish.

Some Fish Glow Brightly

In the deep sea, many fish produce their own light through a process called bioluminescence. They use this glow to attract prey, confuse predators, or find mates. Some have glowing spots under their eyes or along their bodies. Because sunlight can't reach those depths, glowing in the dark becomes a vital survival tool.

Crabs Walk Sideways Only

Most crabs have legs that are jointed in a way that makes sideways movement easier than walking forward or backward. This strange-looking shuffle helps them stay fast and stable on sand or rocky terrain. It's not just a funny dance move, it's a practical way to survive when you have a flat body and a hard shell.

Owls Can't Move Eyes

Unlike humans, owls can't move their eyes from side to side. Their eyes are fixed in place, like binoculars. To see in different directions, they have to move their entire head. Luckily, their necks are super flexible and can rotate about 270 degrees. That's why owls always look like they're staring deep into your soul.

Octopuses Have Three Hearts

An octopus has one heart that keeps blood flowing to the body and two that pump blood to the gills. But here's the weird part: when an octopus starts swimming, the two gill hearts actually stop. That's why octopuses prefer crawling to swimming, it's less exhausting. Imagine if your heart took a coffee break every time you went for a jog.

Penguins Propose with Pebbles

Some male penguins search beaches for the smoothest, shiniest pebble they can find. When they spot a potential mate, they present the pebble as a sort of engagement gift. If the female accepts, she places it in her nest. No rings, no flowers, just a really good rock. It's nature's cutest version of popping the question.

Flamingos Get Pink from Food

A group of flamingos is called a "flamboyance." And honestly, what else would you call a bunch of hot pink birds standing on one leg, looking like runway models with attitude? Flamingos aren't just fabulous by name, they also get their color from the shrimp and algae they eat. Without that diet, they'd be a boring gray. So yes, even flamingos are living proof that you are what you eat.

Food & Drink

Bananas Are Radioactive

Bananas contain potassium and a tiny part of that potassium is a radioactive isotope called potassium-40. But don't worry, you'd need to eat thousands of bananas in one sitting to feel any effects. Scientists actually use the "banana equivalent dose" to explain small amounts of radiation in everyday life. So yes, your snack glows a little but in the safest way possible.

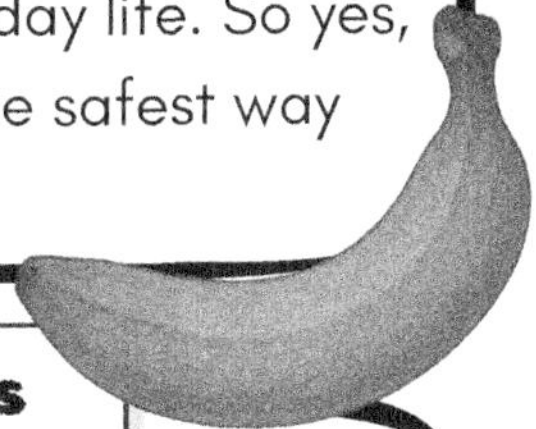

Honey Never Goes Bad

Archaeologists have found pots of honey in ancient Egyptian tombs that are over 3,000 years old and still perfectly edible. Honey's low moisture content and natural acidity make it an unfriendly place for bacteria. That means honey basically lasts forever. It's the only food that truly doesn't expire, which makes it both delicious and kind of immortal.

Pineapples Eat You Back

Pineapples contain an enzyme called bromelain, which breaks down proteins. When you eat fresh pineapple, that enzyme starts breaking down the proteins in your mouth. That's why your tongue sometimes feels sore or tingly after eating it. Don't worry, your mouth heals quickly. But technically, while you're eating pineapple, it's also nibbling on you.

Carrots Used To Be Purple

The first cultivated carrots were purple, yellow, or white. The orange variety didn't appear until the 1600s in the Netherlands, possibly in honor of the royal House of Orange. Farmers selectively bred them for the bright color we know today. So next time you crunch on a carrot, remember it's the result of centuries of veggie fashion trends.

Cheese Was Probably An Accident

Historians believe cheese was discovered when someone stored milk in a container made from an animal's stomach, which contained natural enzymes. The milk curdled and turned into something thicker, tastier and longer-lasting. That ancient mistake eventually led to the creation of thousands of cheese types we enjoy today. Thank you, random ancient person with weird storage habits.

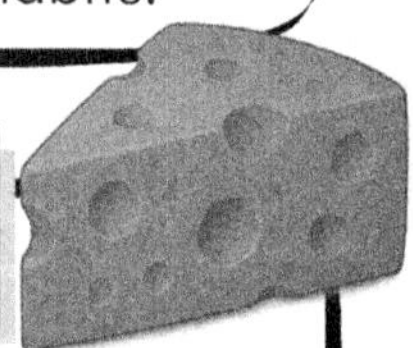

Tomatoes Were Feared

In 18th-century Europe, many people thought tomatoes were poisonous. This wasn't completely irrational because tomatoes are part of the nightshade family, which includes some toxic plants. The tomato wasn't cleared of suspicion until much later, when people realized it was delicious, not deadly.

Popsicles Were Invented By Accident

In 1905, an 11-year-old boy named Frank Epperson accidentally left a cup of soda with a stirring stick outside on a freezing night. By morning, it was frozen solid. He pulled it out and tasted it and the popsicle was born. He didn't patent the idea until years later, but his chilly mistake became one of the world's most beloved summer treats.

Cucumbers Are Mostly Water

Cucumbers are about 96 percent water, making them one of the most hydrating foods you can eat. That's why they're often used in spa treatments and refreshing summer dishes. They're technically fruits, not vegetables and they've been cultivated for over 3,000 years. Crisp, cool and practically a drink in solid form.

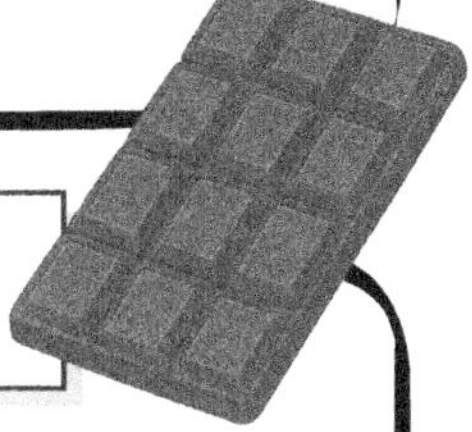

Chocolate Was Once Money

The ancient Maya and Aztec peoples valued cacao so highly that they used it as currency. Cacao beans could buy food, clothes, or even pay taxes. They also made a bitter chocolate drink used in ceremonies. Sweet chocolate as we know it didn't appear until much later, after sugar was added in Europe. Imagine buying a snack with a snack.

Bread Was Baked In Space

In 2015, astronauts on the International Space Station baked the first bread in space using a special zero-gravity oven. Before that, bread crumbs were too risky because they could float into equipment. The space-friendly version used a tortilla-like dough. It wasn't just a fun experiment, it helped researchers understand how cooking might work on future Mars missions.

Mushrooms Are Not Plants

Mushrooms might look like plants, but they belong to an entirely different group called fungi. They don't use sunlight to grow and instead break down organic matter around them. Some glow in the dark, some are used in medicine and some can even survive in radioactive zones. They're one of the strangest foods on the planet.

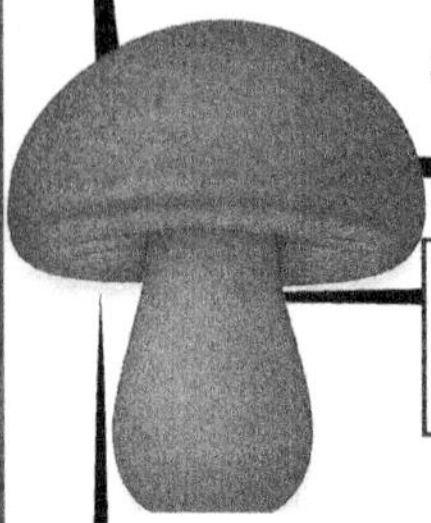

Lemons Float, Limes Sink

Even though lemons and limes look similar, only lemons float in water. That's because lemons have a slightly thicker rind and more air pockets inside, making them less dense. Limes are just heavy enough to sink. It's a tiny difference, but a great party trick and a fun way to tell them apart.

Peanuts Aren't Real Nuts

Peanuts grow underground and belong to the legume family, just like beans and lentils. Real nuts, like almonds and walnuts, grow on trees. The name "peanut" stuck anyway and most people never question it. So the next time someone offers you a nut, you can impress them with a little underground knowledge.

Potatoes Went To Space

Potatoes were the first vegetables grown in space under controlled conditions. In the 1990s, NASA teamed up with agricultural scientists to test how food could be grown on other planets. Potatoes were chosen because they're hardy, nutritious and can grow in limited space. They might just be our future food on Mars.

Watermelons Are From Africa

Watermelons were first grown in northeastern Africa over 4,000 years ago. Ancient Egyptians even drew them on the walls of tombs. Back then, they weren't as sweet as today's versions, but they were prized for their water content. Over centuries, farmers bred them to be juicier and redder. Now they're the ultimate summer fruit, but they started as desert hydration tools.

Milk Helps With Spicy Food

If you eat something too spicy, water won't help much, it just spreads the heat around. Milk, however, contains a protein called casein that breaks down capsaicin, the chemical that makes chili peppers burn. That's why dairy products like yogurt or cheese can cool your mouth faster than a glass of water ever could.

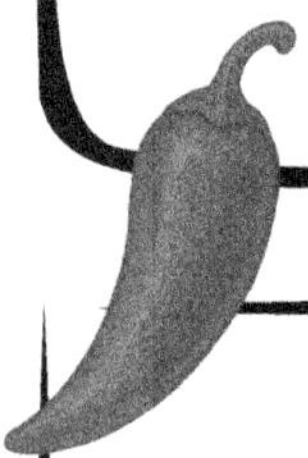

Salt Used To Be Valuable

In ancient times, salt was so important for preserving food that it was often used like money. Roman soldiers were sometimes paid in salt, which is where the word "salary" comes from. Even entire trade routes were built around it. Today it's cheap and common, but centuries ago, it was a life-saver and a status symbol.

Pufferfish Can Be Food

In Japan, the pufferfish—called fugu—is considered a delicacy, but it's also one of the most dangerous meals in the world. The fish contains a deadly toxin and only specially trained chefs are allowed to prepare it. If not done correctly, it can be fatal. Despite the risk, it remains popular among brave food lovers who trust their chefs completely.

Ice Cream Was Once Rare

Before refrigerators, ice cream was a luxury enjoyed mostly by the rich. Making it required natural ice, special storage and lots of time. In the 1600s and 1700s, it was a royal treat. It wasn't until the 20th century, with the rise of refrigeration and mass production, that it became a treat anyone could enjoy.

Some Cheeses Smell Awful

Certain cheeses like Limburger or Époisses are known for their incredibly strong smell. The bacteria used in the fermentation process is the same type found on human skin, especially between toes. That's why some cheeses smell like feet. Despite the odor, many of them taste mild and creamy. Smelly on the outside, heavenly on the inside.

Instant Noodles Were Invented After War

Instant noodles were created in Japan in 1958 by Momofuku Ando, who wanted to make a cheap, convenient food to help feed the population after World War II. His invention quickly spread across the world. Today, billions of servings are eaten every year, especially by students, travelers and anyone on a budget.

Coffee Beans Aren't Beans

Coffee "beans" are actually the seeds of the coffee fruit, which looks like a red or purple cherry. Once harvested, the outer fruit is removed and the seed is roasted to become what we know as a coffee bean. So while we call them beans, they're really just pit-roasted fruit seeds that power millions of mornings.

Ketchup Was Once Medicine

In the 1830s, ketchup was sold as a cure for indigestion. A doctor even turned it into pill form and marketed it as a health remedy. Back then, it was made mostly from mushrooms and fish, not tomatoes. Today it's just a tasty topping, but for a short time, people actually took it like medicine.

Chili Peppers Trick Your Brain

When you eat spicy food, your mouth isn't actually burning. The heat comes from a chemical called capsaicin, which tricks your brain into thinking you're in danger. That's why your body reacts by sweating, crying, or turning red. It's fake pain but your brain doesn't know that. The result? A fiery thrill with every bite.

You Can Drink Maple Sap

Before maple sap is boiled into syrup, it can be drunk straight from the tree. It tastes slightly sweet and refreshing and some people collect it each spring as a natural drink. It contains water, minerals and a touch of sugar. While it's not as sweet as syrup, it's a fun and traditional way to enjoy nature's candy.

Rice Feeds Half The World

Rice is the main food for more than half of the world's population. It's grown in over 100 countries and comes in thousands of varieties. From sushi in Japan to curries in India and stir-fries in China, rice plays a central role in many cultures. It's one of the most important crops in human history.

Bread Rises With Tiny Farts

Yeast, the fungus used to make bread rise, eats sugar in the dough and releases gas as a result. These tiny gas bubbles are what make the dough puff up and become soft and airy. So yes, your loaf of bread is full of millions of microscopic yeast farts. Delicious, fluffy and slightly gross. Just how we like it.

Corn Can Grow Super Fast

Under perfect conditions, corn can grow more than 60 centimeters in a single week. That's almost like watching it stretch before your eyes. Farmers have even reported hearing popping sounds from fields as corn rapidly expands. It's one of the reasons corn is such a powerful crop: fast, versatile and everywhere from snacks to fuel.

Coconut Water Saves Lives

In emergencies, coconut water has been used as a substitute for IV fluid because it's sterile inside the shell and has similar properties to human plasma. This isn't common today, but it's been done during wartime when supplies ran out. While not a long-term solution, it shows just how unique and useful nature can be.

Sugar Used To Be Rare

For centuries, sugar was so expensive that only the rich could afford it. It was considered a luxury and people used it sparingly in medicine or special desserts. It wasn't until sugarcane plantations spread and production increased that sugar became common. Now it's everywhere, but it once symbolized wealth and status.

Spaghetti Trees Fooled Viewers

In 1957, a British TV station aired a fake news segment showing people harvesting spaghetti from trees. Many viewers believed it. The prank became one of the most famous April Fool's jokes in TV history. It worked because pasta wasn't widely known in the UK at the time, so the idea didn't seem completely impossible.

Marshmallows Were Once Medicinal

The original marshmallow was made from the root of the marshmallow plant and used to soothe sore throats. The modern version is pure sugar and gelatin, with no plant left in sight. But the name stuck. What began as herbal medicine is now a campfire classic that melts perfectly over chocolate and graham crackers.

Eating Snow Isn't Hydrating

While snow is made of water, eating it can actually make you colder and use up energy your body needs to stay warm. In survival situations, it's better to melt snow before drinking it. It may look like a free drink from the sky, but it's not always helpful when you're trying to stay alive.

Vanilla Comes From Orchids

Real vanilla flavoring comes from the seed pods of a tropical orchid. The process of growing and harvesting it is slow and labor-intensive, which is why natural vanilla is so expensive. Most vanilla-flavored products today use synthetic vanillin instead. Still, the real thing remains one of the most loved flavors on Earth.

Bubble Gum Was A Mistake

The first successful bubble gum was invented in 1928 by a man named Walter Diemer, who was trying to improve chewing gum. He accidentally created a stretchy formula that allowed people to blow bubbles. He dyed it pink because it was the only color he had. That's why pink is still the classic gum color today.

French Fries Aren't French

Despite the name, French fries likely originated in Belgium, where villagers were frying potatoes as early as the 1600s. American soldiers during World War I called them "French" because French was the local language. The name stuck, but Belgians still take credit for inventing one of the world's favorite side dishes.

Pop
Culture

Mickey Mouse Had Rivals

When Mickey Mouse became popular in the 1930s, other studios rushed to create their own cartoon animals. Some, like Felix the Cat and Oswald the Lucky Rabbit, came close to stealing the spotlight. But Disney doubled down on Mickey's personality and marketing, eventually making him one of the most famous characters of all time. His biggest rival? Probably Bugs Bunny.

LEGO Means Play Well

The name LEGO comes from the Danish words "leg godt," which mean "play well." The company started as a wooden toy maker in 1932 before inventing the plastic bricks we know today. Now LEGO is one of the biggest toy brands in the world, with movies, theme parks, and even sets designed by fans.

Barbie Has Over 200 Careers

Barbie has done almost every job imaginable. Since her debut in 1959, she's been an astronaut, doctor, pilot, firefighter, president and more. The idea was always that girls could be anything they wanted. Barbie even went to space before real American women did, thanks to her 1965 astronaut edition.

Harry Potter Was Rejected

Before becoming a global success, the Harry Potter manuscript was rejected by 12 different publishers. One even told the author that children wouldn't want to read a book that long. Eventually, a small publishing house took the risk. The series went on to sell over 500 million copies and inspire movies, theme parks and generations of readers.

TikTok Came From China

TikTok was created by a Chinese tech company called ByteDance in 2016. It started as an app called Douyin in China, then launched internationally as TikTok. With its short videos, music and trends, it became one of the fastest-growing social platforms in history, changing how people express themselves online.

Walt Disney Voiced Mickey

In the early years, Walt Disney himself provided the voice for Mickey Mouse. He continued doing it for almost two decades. It was his way of staying personally connected to the character that launched his empire. Later, professional voice actors took over, but Walt's voice was Mickey's first.

The Beatles Failed Auditions

Before becoming legends, The Beatles were rejected by several record labels. One company even said guitar music was "on the way out." They eventually signed with a small label called Parlophone. The rest is music history. It's a reminder that even the biggest stars hear "no" before they get a "yes."

Pixar Almost Shut Down

Before Toy Story was released in 1995, Pixar was struggling financially. The company had tried several directions, including making hardware and short films. Toy Story's success saved the studio and started a wave of hit animated movies. Without that one big risk, Pixar might not exist today.

Star Wars Changed Everything

When Star Wars premiered in 1977, no one expected it to be a global phenomenon. But it broke box office records and changed how movies were made and marketed. It introduced the blockbuster era, sparked merchandise empires and created a universe that fans still explore today: on screen, in books and at conventions.

Scooby-Doo Fought Censorship

Scooby-Doo was created in 1969 after parents complained that children's cartoons were too violent. The idea was to mix mystery with comedy instead of action. The show became a hit and proved that spooky stories could be funny too. It also introduced the classic format of "a villain in a mask"—something still copied today.

Frozen Broke Song Records

The song "Let It Go" from Disney's Frozen became a global sensation. It won an Oscar, topped charts and was translated into dozens of languages. The movie's soundtrack became one of the best-selling animated soundtracks ever. Whether you love it or can't hear it one more time, it's one of the most iconic songs in animation.

Pokémon Means Pocket Monsters

Pokémon began in Japan as a video game about capturing small creatures. The name comes from the words "pocket" and "monsters." What started as a Game Boy game turned into a massive franchise with trading cards, TV shows, movies and merchandise. With hundreds of creatures and millions of fans, it became a pop culture giant.

Barcodes Were First Used On Gum

The first product ever scanned with a barcode was a pack of chewing gum in 1974. This simple invention changed the way stores track inventory and check out purchases. Today, barcodes are on almost everything you buy. And it all started with a stick of gum in Ohio.

Marvel Almost Sold Spider-Man

In the 1990s, Marvel was struggling and tried to sell film rights to several characters. One studio agreed to buy only Spider-Man and passed on the rest, saying no one cared about other heroes. That mistake led to Marvel creating its own film universe years later with characters like Iron Man and Thor and building a multi-billion-dollar franchise.

Minecraft Was Made By One

The first version of Minecraft was created by a single Swedish developer named Markus Persson in just a few weeks. He kept adding features and released it online. Players loved the freedom to build and explore. The game became so popular that Microsoft later bought it for over 2 billion dollars. Not bad for a pixel world.

Super Mario Was A Carpenter

When Mario first appeared in the 1981 video game Donkey Kong, he wasn't a plumber yet—he was a carpenter named Jumpman. His look was designed to fit the simple graphics: a hat so animators didn't have to draw hair and a mustache to show his nose. He became a plumber later when the game moved to pipes.

Spotify Was Launched In Sweden

Spotify, the music streaming giant, started in Sweden in 2008. The goal was to fight music piracy by making legal music more convenient than downloading illegally. It quickly changed how people listen to music around the world. Now millions of songs are just one tap away—no CD, no download, no problem.

The Simpsons Broke Records

The Simpsons is the longest-running American scripted TV show. It began in 1989 and has produced over 700 episodes. It's known for predicting real-life events, from tech inventions to political moments. With its yellow skin and endless jokes, it has become a true pop culture icon across generations.

Hello Kitty Has No Mouth

Hello Kitty is one of the most recognizable characters in the world but she doesn't have a mouth. The creators said this helps people imagine their own feelings through her face. She was introduced in 1974 and has appeared on everything from school supplies to airplanes. With no voice and no mouth, she still says a lot.

Tetris Was Invented In Russia

Tetris was created by a Russian computer engineer in 1984. It became popular worldwide when it was bundled with the original Game Boy. The game's simple rules and addictive style made it one of the most played video games of all time. It also inspired research into how games affect the brain.

Disney Almost Lost Mickey

In the early days, Walt Disney didn't copyright Mickey Mouse properly. Another studio nearly took the character away. That experience taught Disney the importance of protecting his work. Since then, Disney has carefully guarded Mickey's image and helped change copyright laws in the process. Mickey became both a mascot and a legal milestone.

The Moon Landing Was Televised

When Apollo 11 landed on the Moon in 1969, over 600 million people watched it live on TV. It was the largest broadcast event in history at the time. Neil Armstrong's words "one small step for man" became part of pop culture. The broadcast helped turn astronauts into global celebrities.

Game Shows Use Trickery

Many game shows use subtle techniques to increase drama. Lights are dimmed during tense moments and music builds suspense. Some shows even film fake reaction shots after the episode to improve editing. The prizes are real but the tension is carefully planned. What looks spontaneous is often tightly scripted behind the scenes.

Rihanna Ignored The Super Bowl

Rihanna was once asked if she'd perform at the Super Bowl. Her answer: "Not until I feel like it." Then she surprised the world by agreeing years later and performed while pregnant, floating on a moving platform above the stage. People didn't know whether to cheer or panic. So they did both.

How the Oscars Got Named

The official name is the Academy Awards, but "Oscar" became popular after someone said the golden statue looked like her uncle Oscar. The nickname stuck and became the common term worldwide. Today, the Oscars are one of the most-watched events in entertainment, even though they've changed a lot since they began in 1929.

Elvis Was Rejected Too

Before becoming the King of Rock and Roll, Elvis Presley was told he would never make it in music. One early manager told him to go back to truck driving. But his unique voice and energetic performances soon proved everyone wrong. He became a global icon and changed the music industry forever.

SpongeBob Was A Real Pitch

SpongeBob SquarePants was created by a marine biologist who wanted to make an educational cartoon. The idea was originally called "SpongeBoy Ahoy" and featured facts about ocean life. While it turned into a goofy comedy, the characters and settings still reflect real sea creatures and underwater details. Bikini Bottom is even based on a real place.

Beyoncé Broke Grammy Records

Beyoncé has won more Grammy Awards than any other singer in history. Her performances, videos and lyrics are often carefully planned to include hidden meanings, references and symbolism. She also helped shape modern pop music by blending different styles and pushing creative boundaries with each new album.

Godzilla Has A Star

Godzilla, the giant movie monster from Japan, has a star on the Hollywood Walk of Fame. The character first appeared in 1954 and became a symbol of both destruction and survival. Over the years, Godzilla starred in dozens of films and even fought King Kong. Not bad for a radioactive lizard in a rubber suit.

Oprah Was Once Fired

Before becoming one of the most powerful women in media, Oprah Winfrey was fired from her first TV news job. She was told she was too emotional for news reporting. Instead of quitting, she focused on building a talk show where emotion was her strength. That show became a global success and helped redefine television.

Instagram Changed Food Forever

Before social media, people didn't usually photograph their meals. But Instagram turned food into content. Restaurants now design dishes to look good in photos and entire careers were built around sharing recipes and snack reviews. A meal is no longer just food, it's often a photo opportunity too.

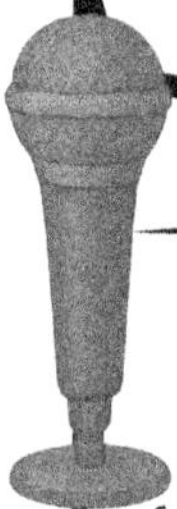

Adele Forgot Her Lyrics

During a huge concert, Adele once completely forgot the words to her own song and just started laughing. The audience sang it for her while she recovered. She's known for turning mistakes into charming moments and often talks casually with the crowd like they're old friends, which makes her even more lovable.

Justin Bieber's Career Started On YouTube

Justin Bieber's rise started with homemade videos on YouTube, where he covered songs as a kid. A talent manager stumbled upon them and reached out. Just a few months later, Bieber was recording music with Usher. One day he was in school — the next, he was performing in front of millions of screaming fans.

Grumpy Cat Made Millions

Grumpy Cat, whose real name was Tardar Sauce, became famous for her permanently angry-looking face. After one viral photo, she landed TV spots, her own merchandise and even a movie. Despite her expression, she was apparently sweet in real life. And worth more than most celebrities.

Lady Gaga Wore Meat

At an awards show, Lady Gaga wore a dress made entirely of raw meat. It sparked massive media attention, memes, and debate. Gaga said it was a protest about personal rights. Whatever the reason, it instantly became one of the most unforgettable red carpet moments in pop culture history.

Will Smith Was Broke

Before The Fresh Prince of Bel-Air, Will Smith had blown all his money and owed the IRS thousands. He took the role on the condition that most of his paychecks would go to the government. Within a year, he was famous again and back on top, proving that even cool guys make bad money choices.

Science &
Technology

Concrete Gets Stronger Over Time

Unlike many materials that wear down, concrete actually continues to strengthen for years after it is poured. The process is called curing and it happens as the material reacts with water. That is why ancient Roman concrete structures are still standing while some modern buildings crumble.

The Internet Has Weight

In theory, the electrons that carry the entire internet's data have a combined weight about the same as a strawberry. That is how tiny data is on a particle level. So all the videos, emails, games, and cat memes you have ever seen online exist as something you could balance on your toast.

Robots Have Citizenship

In 2017, a humanoid robot named Sophia was granted legal citizenship by Saudi Arabia. She can hold conversations, make jokes, and even express facial emotions. It was part marketing, part science experiment, but it made her the first robot in the world with a passport and a press tour.

Tires Used To Be White

Early car tires were pure white because rubber is naturally light in color. Then carbon black was added to make them stronger and more durable. It also turned them black, which is now the standard. So that dark tire color we all know is just a side effect of chemistry.

3D Printing Builds Organs

Scientists are using 3D printers to create human body parts like ears and skin. In some labs, researchers are even printing cells that could grow into organs. The goal is to one day print replacement parts for people using their own DNA. It sounds like science fiction but it is happening right now.

Insects Inspired Drones

Scientists have studied how flies and bees move to design flying robots. Their wings flap in complex patterns that make them stable and fast. By copying these motions, engineers have built small drones that can hover, zip through tight spaces, and even pollinate plants.

Metal Can Remember Shapes

Shape memory alloys are metals that can be bent or twisted and will snap back into their original shape when heated. Scientists use them in medical devices, space tech, and even eyeglass frames. It is like giving metal a memory. You bend it, heat it, and it acts like nothing ever happened.

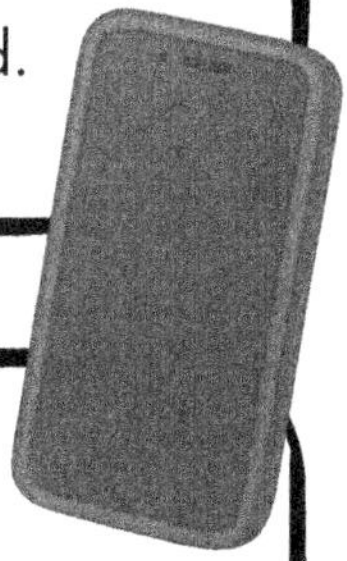

Your Phone Is Super Powerful

The smartphone in your hand is more powerful than the computers that took astronauts to the moon. The Apollo missions ran on systems with less processing power than a digital watch today. Your phone could run circles around them if it were not too busy playing videos and checking messages.

Failed Rubber

A failed attempt to make rubber led to the invention of one of the strongest glues ever made. Chemists were trying to create a clear plastic for gun sights. Instead, they made something so sticky it bonded to everything. It was useless at first until someone realized how useful that was.

A Day Is Not Perfect

A day is not exactly 24 hours. Earth spins once every 23 hours and 56 minutes. The reason we call it 24 is because of the way Earth moves around the sun. We add a little bit of time each day to keep calendars in sync. That is also why we need leap years.

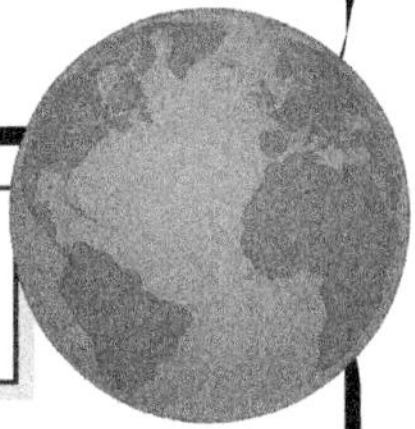

Plants Can Hear Sounds

Studies show that plants react to certain sounds. For example, some flowers open faster when they sense the buzzing of bees. Others change how they grow based on vibrations in the soil. Plants do not have ears but they can sense pressure and react in ways that still seem like science fiction.

Ants Do Farm Work

Certain species of ants grow their own food by farming fungus. They cut leaves, carry them home, and feed them to the fungus, which grows in their nests. Then they eat the fungus. These tiny farmers even have special ants that clean the crops and protect them from pests.

Early Computers Filled Rooms

The first general-purpose computer was so big it filled an entire room and weighed over 25 tons. It could only solve one problem at a time and had no screen. Today, the phone in your pocket is millions of times more powerful than those room-sized machines.

Lasers Can Move Clouds

Scientists have experimented with using lasers to create tiny sparks in the sky that could trigger rain. The technology is not fully developed but the idea is to control weather in small areas. It is called cloud seeding and it has already been done using airplanes, but lasers might be next.

Octopus Skin Sees Light

An octopus can change color without using its eyes. Its skin has light-sensitive cells that help it detect changes in brightness and adjust accordingly. This gives it a second way to camouflage, even if it cannot see what is behind it. It is like having eyes all over your body.

Airplanes Were Invented Twice

The Wright brothers are credited with the first successful airplane flight in 1903. But a Brazilian man named Alberto Santos-Dumont also built and flew a plane around the same time. He is considered the inventor of the airplane in some countries. Sometimes history gives credit based on publicity, not just performance.

Birds Are Living Dinosaurs

Modern birds evolved from a group of small meat-eating dinosaurs. That means when you see a pigeon or parrot, you are basically looking at a tiny dinosaur with feathers. Scientists even found fossils of dinosaurs with wings and beaks. The age of dinosaurs never really ended, it just got fluffier.

Your Body Glows Slightly

Humans naturally emit a very faint glow, but it is about 1,000 times too dim for our eyes to see. Scientists using special cameras have captured this light coming from the face, chest, and hands. It is caused by chemical reactions in our cells. So yes, your body shines a little, just not enough to light a room.

Magnets Can Levitate Frogs

In a famous experiment, scientists used a powerful magnet to levitate a frog. The magnetic field affected the water inside its body and lifted it into the air. The frog was unharmed and floated peacefully. The same method has been used to levitate strawberries and even drops of water.

Electric Eels Can Charge Batteries

Electric eels produce electricity to shock prey and defend themselves. In labs, scientists have connected them to tiny power systems and lit up LEDs. It is not enough to charge a phone yet but it shows how living creatures can create usable energy. Nature has some strange generators.

A Year Is Not Precise

A calendar year is 365 days but Earth actually takes about 365.24 days to orbit the sun. That is why we add an extra day every four years. Without leap years, the seasons would slowly shift out of sync and summer would eventually happen in December.

Some Metals Explode In Water

Metals like sodium and potassium react violently when dropped into water. They fizz, spark and can even explode. The reaction is so strong that science teachers often use it for dramatic experiments. It is fun to watch in a lab, but never something to try at home.

You Are Mostly Empty Space

If you removed all the space inside your atoms, your body could be compressed to the size of a grain of rice. That is because atoms are made of tiny particles with lots of empty space between them. Matter seems solid but it is mostly nothing.

Whales Have Finger Bones

Inside a whale's flippers are bones that look just like human fingers. That is because whales and land mammals share a common ancestor. Over millions of years, those fingers became adapted for swimming. It is a strange but beautiful example of evolution hiding in plain sight.

Water Can Boil And Freeze At The Same Time

Under the right conditions in space, water can boil and freeze at the same time. This happens when there is almost no air pressure. The liquid turns into vapor and ice simultaneously. It sounds impossible on Earth but in a vacuum, the rules of physics get weird fast.

Some Computers Run On Water

Researchers have built computers that use droplets of water to carry out basic logic functions. These water-based systems are incredibly slow but they demonstrate how information can move in surprising ways. It is not practical for your phone but it helps us think outside the chip.

Jellyfish Can Live Forever

One species of jellyfish can revert to its younger form after becoming an adult. It does this by cycling its cells backward and starting life over again. In theory, this process could repeat forever. Scientists are studying it to understand aging and maybe one day slow it down in humans.

Bacteria Talk To Each Other

Bacteria use chemical signals to communicate in a process called quorum sensing. They release molecules that let them sense how many others are nearby. Once enough of them gather, they start acting together like forming a biofilm or attacking a host. It is like a tiny microbial group chat.

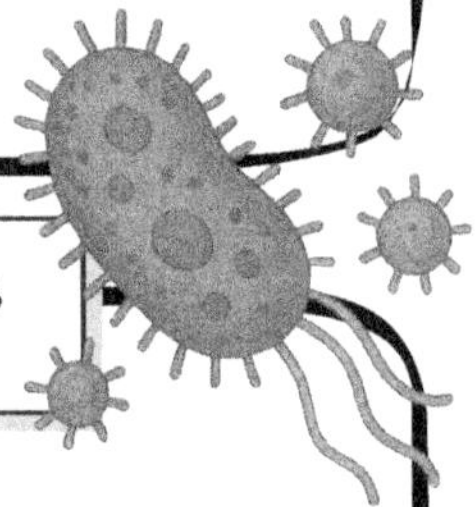

Microwaves Were A Mistake

The microwave oven was invented after a scientist noticed that a candy bar in his pocket melted near radar equipment. He realized the waves were heating the chocolate and tested them on popcorn next. It worked so well that the kitchen microwave was born from pure accident.

Velcro Came From Nature

Velcro was invented after a Swiss engineer noticed burrs stuck to his dog's fur. Under a microscope, he saw tiny hooks that clung to loops of hair. He copied the idea using fabric and created a new type of fastener. Now it is used in shoes, jackets, and even spacesuits.

You Shed Skin Constantly

Your body sheds about 30,000 to 40,000 skin cells every minute. That means most of the dust in your home is actually made of dead skin. In one year, you lose around four kilograms of skin. Do not worry though, your body is always growing new layers to replace it.

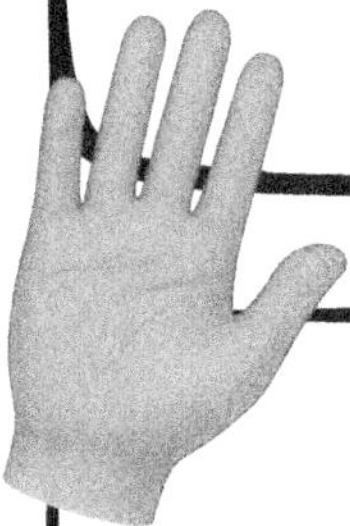

Glass Moves Very Slowly

Old glass windows are often thicker at the bottom than at the top. That led people to believe glass flows over time. In reality, it is just how they were made. But glass is still considered an extremely slow-moving liquid by some scientists, even if it takes centuries to notice.

Some Animals Glow Naturally

Bioluminescence is the ability of living things to produce light. Fireflies are the most famous example but many deep-sea creatures do it too. They use their glow to attract mates, confuse predators, or light up their surroundings. In the ocean, glowing might be more common than not glowing.

Plastic Can Be Made From Milk

In the early 1900s, people made a type of plastic using milk and vinegar. The milk proteins clump together and harden into a solid. This early plastic was used for buttons and jewelry. It is not common today but shows how everyday ingredients can lead to scientific discoveries.

Lasers Can Cut Through Diamonds

Diamonds are the hardest natural material on Earth but they can still be cut using concentrated laser beams. The laser heats and weakens the crystal structure, allowing precise slices. This method is used in both jewelry making and advanced electronics.

Color Printers Hide Tracking Dots

Most color printers leave behind tiny yellow dots on every page they print. These dots contain codes that reveal when and where the page was printed. They are almost invisible to the eye but can be read by special software. It is a built-in way to trace documents for security.

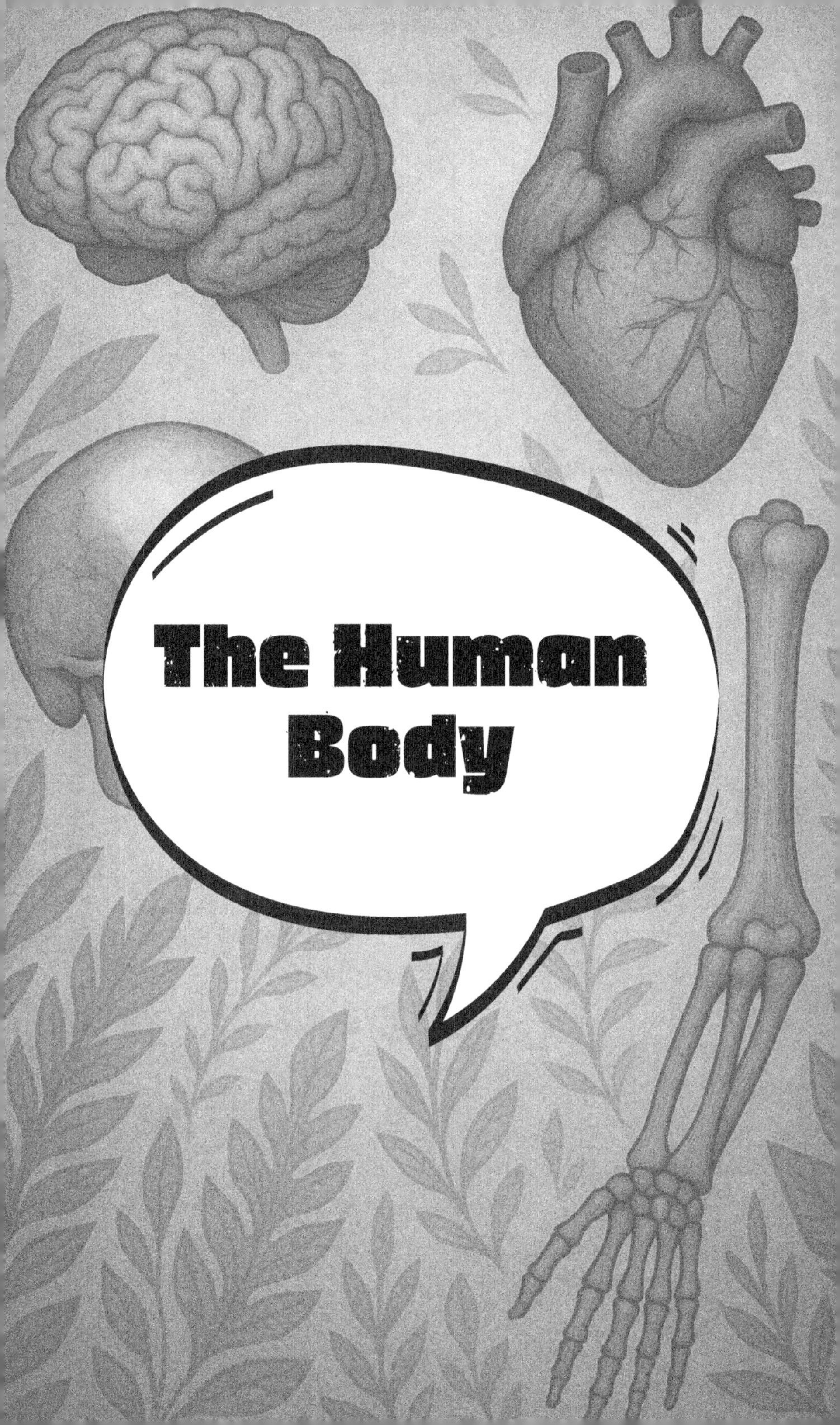
The Human Body

Your Bones Are Wet

Even though bones seem dry and hard, they are filled with living tissue and fluid. Inside is a spongy material called marrow, which helps produce blood cells. Bones are actually organs, not just support structures. That means your skeleton is alive and working every single day.

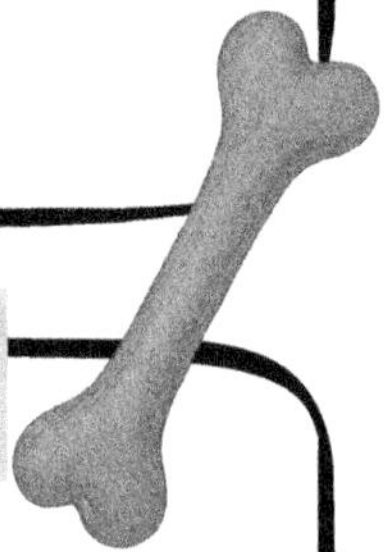

Hair Grows After Death

People used to believe that hair and nails grow after death, but what really happens is that the skin dries out and shrinks. This makes hair and nails appear longer. It is an optical illusion caused by dehydration, not a creepy afterlife effect.

Your Tongue Is Unique

Just like fingerprints, no two people have the same tongue print. The shape, texture, and pattern of your tongue are completely your own. Scientists have even studied tongue prints for use in security systems, although licking your way through a password would be pretty weird.

You Make Saliva Daily

Your mouth produces up to two liters of saliva per day. That is enough to fill a large soda bottle. Saliva helps break down food, protect teeth, and even heal wounds. Without it, chewing and speaking would be a lot more difficult.

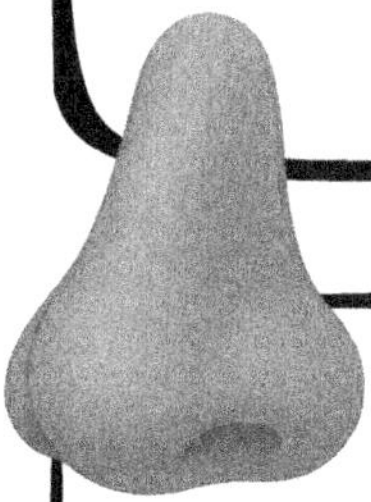

Your Nose Can Remember Smells

The human nose can detect over one trillion different scents. Your brain stores smell memories, which is why a single scent can bring back strong emotions. Smell is directly linked to the emotional center of the brain, more than sight or sound.

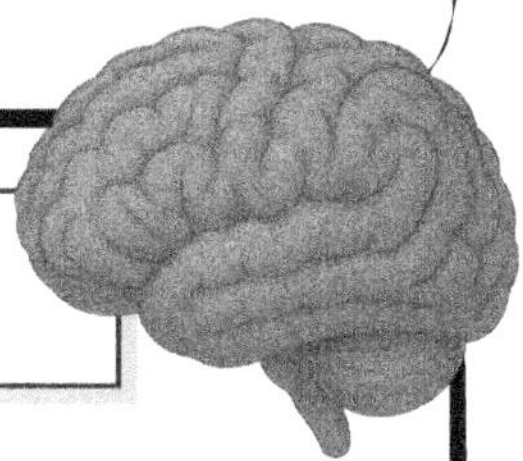

You Have Two "Brains"

Your digestive system has its own complex network of nerves called the enteric nervous system. It controls digestion independently and communicates with your actual brain. Scientists sometimes call it the second brain, and it is one reason your gut feelings are often surprisingly accurate.

You Blink A Lot

The average person blinks around 15 to 20 times per minute. That adds up to more than 20,000 times a day. Blinking keeps your eyes clean and moist, and it also gives your brain tiny breaks while reading or watching something. It is like a built-in screen saver for your vision.

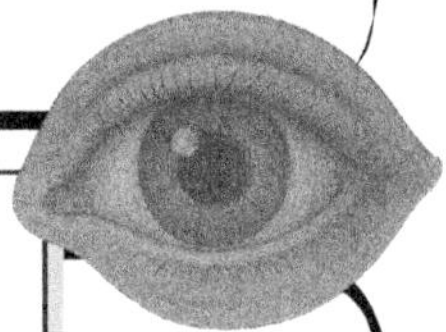

You Cannot Swallow And Breathe

It is physically impossible to swallow and breathe at the same time. That is because both actions use the same passage in your throat. A flap called the epiglottis closes during swallowing to keep food out of your lungs. That little flap keeps you from choking every time you eat.

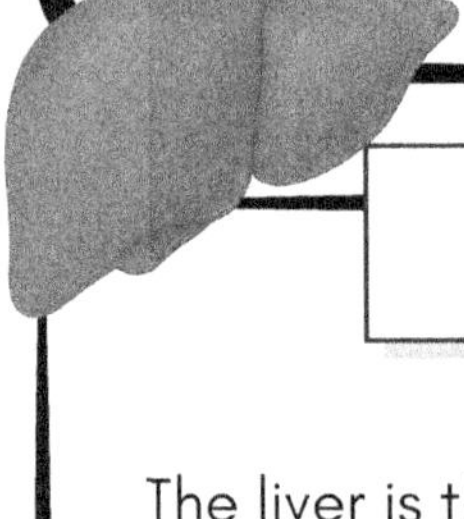

Your Liver Can Regrow

The liver is the only organ in your body that can regenerate. Even if two thirds of it are removed, it can grow back to full size. This makes liver transplants more flexible, and some people donate just part of their liver to help others survive.

Your Brain Rewrites Memories

Every time you recall a memory, your brain slightly alters it. The process of remembering activates similar brain regions as imagining or dreaming. Over time, your memories shift, blur, or even gain false details. So the more often you remember something, the less accurate it may become.

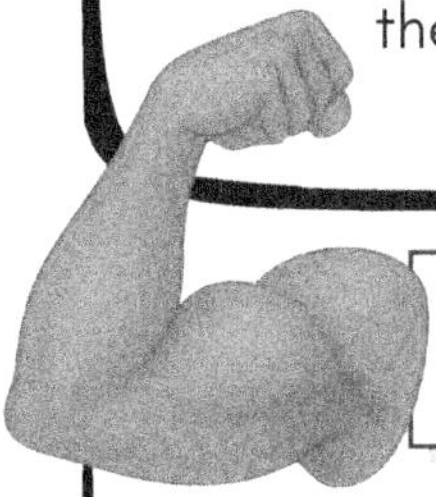

Muscles Store Emotional Stress

Tension is not just in your mind. Emotional stress often shows up physically, especially in muscles like the neck, shoulders, and jaw. The body can hold patterns of stress long after the trigger is gone. That is why techniques like breathwork and stretching can help you process emotions without saying a word.

You Smell Through Your Brain

Unlike other senses, smell bypasses the usual brain pathways and goes straight to the limbic system, where emotions and memories live. That is why smells can instantly trigger flashbacks or deep feelings. No other sense has such a direct emotional link.

Your Skeleton Rebuilds Constantly

Every seven to ten years, your entire skeleton is replaced. Old bone cells are broken down and new ones are built in their place. This process slows with age, but it continues throughout life. So technically, the bones in your body today are not the ones you had a decade ago.

You Can Train Pain Response

Pain is not just physical. The brain filters and shapes how pain is experienced. Techniques like mindfulness, breathing, or reframing can actually reduce perceived pain by changing how the brain processes signals. Athletes and chronic pain patients often use this to train their nervous system.

You Have A Body Clock

Your circadian rhythm controls not just sleep, but hormone levels, digestion, mood, and even body temperature. Light exposure resets it daily, which is why jet lag and late-night screens can make you feel terrible. Every cell in your body follows this internal schedule, not just your brain.

Goosebumps Are Evolution's Leftover

Goosebumps are caused by tiny muscles pulling on hair follicles. In animals, this fluffs up fur for warmth or intimidation. In humans, it is mostly useless, but still triggered by cold, fear, or emotional moments. It is one of many traits we inherited but no longer really need.

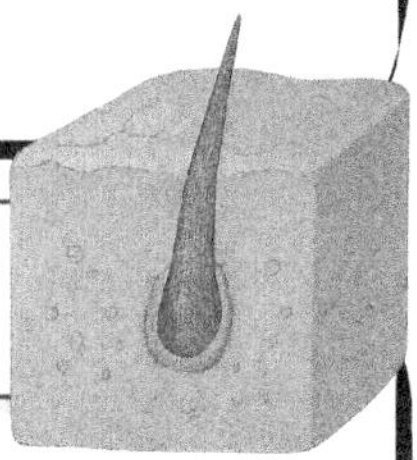

Your Gut Talks To Your Brain

The gut has over 100 million nerve cells and produces more than 90 percent of the body's serotonin. This gut-brain axis affects mood, decision-making, and mental clarity. What you eat influences how you feel, not just physically but emotionally too.

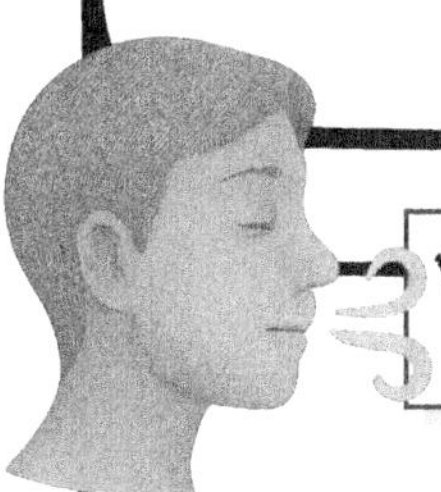

You Breathe Differently When Thinking

Your breathing pattern changes subtly depending on what kind of mental task you are doing. Deep problem-solving often slows your breath while emotional stress speeds it up. Conscious breathing not only reflects your mind's state but can also influence it in return.

Skin Is An Active Organ

Your skin is not just a barrier, it is a complex organ involved in immunity, temperature control, and hormone production. It constantly communicates with the nervous system and even has its own microbiome. What you put on your skin can affect your entire body's balance.

Muscle Memory Is Real

When you stop training, muscles shrink. But the muscle cells keep their nuclei, which act like memory centers. This makes it easier to regain strength later. That is why former athletes or dancers often recover skill and coordination faster after a break than someone starting from zero.

Humans Can Echo-Locate

Some blind individuals have trained themselves to use clicks of the tongue and listen for echoes to detect objects. This skill activates brain regions usually used for vision. It shows how adaptable the brain is and how senses can compensate and reorganize themselves when needed.

The Brain Cannot Feel Pain

Some parts of the brain do not have pain receptors, which means the brain tissue itself cannot feel pain. This is why surgeons can operate on the brain while a patient is awake. Headaches usually come from surrounding structures like blood vessels, nerves, or muscles, not from the brain itself.

You Have A Dominant Nostril

At any given time, one nostril takes in more air than the other. This cycle switches every few hours and helps regulate airflow and smell sensitivity. It is controlled by the autonomic nervous system and most people never notice it, even though it happens all day long.

Your Body Can Taste Water

Until recently, scientists believed water had no taste. But specific receptors on the tongue respond directly to pure water, especially when the mouth is dry. These signals are processed differently from sweet or salty tastes, showing that hydration has its own sensory pathway.

Bones Respond To Sound

Not just ears detect sound, bones can too. This is called bone conduction, and it is how some hearing aids work. Even Beethoven, who lost his hearing, placed a metal rod between his piano and his jawbone so he could feel the music's vibrations. Your skeleton is more acoustically aware than you might expect.

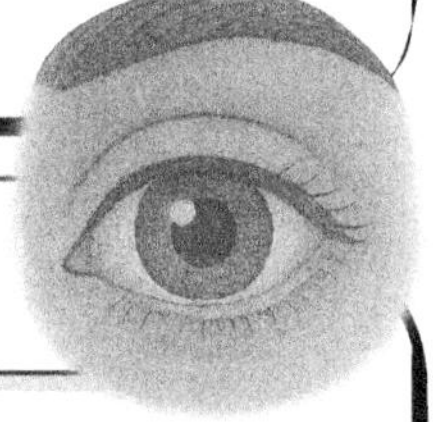

Your Eyes Adjust Constantly

Your pupils do not just react to light. They also change size based on focus, attention, and even emotional state. When you solve a problem or feel surprised, your pupils widen slightly. Your eyes are constantly adapting, even when you do not notice it.

Your Body Reacts Before Thought

The nervous system can trigger reactions before your conscious mind catches up. If you touch something hot, your hand pulls away through a spinal reflex before your brain even registers pain. Your body often makes decisions in milliseconds to protect you.

Fat Is A Complex Organ

Body fat is not just storage. It releases hormones, communicates with your brain, and plays a role in immunity. Scientists now consider it an active endocrine organ. Where fat is stored matters too. Abdominal fat behaves differently than fat under the skin.

Sweat Does Not Smell

Sweat itself is odorless. The smell comes from bacteria on your skin breaking down sweat into acids. Different body areas have different sweat glands, and stress sweat has a different chemical composition than heat sweat, which is why it often smells stronger.

You Shrink During the Day

Throughout the day, gravity compresses the discs between your spine's vertebrae. By evening, you are slightly shorter than in the morning. When you lie down to sleep, the pressure lifts, and your spine returns to full length. The difference is small but measurable.

Blood Moves With Rhythm

Your blood flow is not perfectly steady. It pulses, shifts, and even surges slightly with your breathing. This rhythmic flow helps with oxygen exchange and pressure regulation. Tiny sensors in your body constantly monitor and adjust the system to keep you stable.

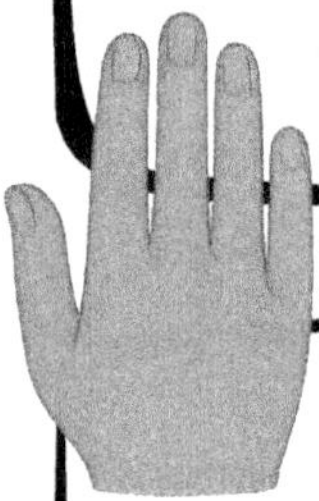

Nails Record Health History

Your fingernails grow slowly and record long-term changes in health. Lines, discoloration, or texture changes can indicate vitamin deficiencies, infections, or stress periods. In some cases, doctors use nail appearance as a diagnostic clue for deeper issues.

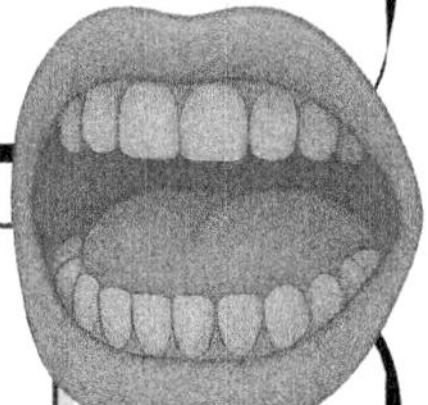

Your Teeth Are Not Bones

Teeth look like bones but are made of different material. They do not contain bone marrow and cannot regenerate. Tooth enamel is the hardest substance in the human body, but once damaged, it does not heal. That is why dentists are so serious about brushing.

You Replace Blood Constantly

Your body produces about two million new red blood cells every second. These cells live around 120 days before being recycled by the spleen. The constant turnover ensures oxygen is delivered efficiently and old cells are cleared out before they become harmful.

Your Spine Is Shock Absorbing

Between the bones of your spine are discs filled with gel-like material that cushion every movement. These intervertebral discs compress when you walk, jump, or sit. Without them, even simple movements would cause pain or damage. They are essential for flexibility and stability.

The Body Has A Default Mode

When your mind is not focused on a task, it shifts into what scientists call the default mode network. This brain state is linked to daydreaming, self-reflection, and creative thinking. Some of your best ideas happen not during focus, but during quiet mental drift.

Geography &
The World

Mount Everest Is Still Growing

Mount Everest rises by a few millimeters every year due to the slow collision of tectonic plates beneath it. The Himalayas were formed when the Indian plate crashed into the Eurasian plate, and the process is still happening. The tallest mountain on Earth is getting even taller.

Africa Has A Snowy Mountain

Despite its hot reputation, Africa is home to Mount Kilimanjaro, which has a snow-covered peak. Located near the equator, the mountain's height allows temperatures cold enough for ice and snow. Climate change is shrinking these glaciers, but for now, snow still exists in the tropics.

Canada Has The Most Lakes

Canada has more natural lakes than any other country in the world. In fact, it holds over half of all the freshwater lakes on Earth. Some are massive, like Lake Superior, while others are small and hidden in forests. Many are so remote they have never been officially named.

The Amazon Has No Bridges

The Amazon River stretches over 6,000 kilometers and passes through multiple countries, but it has no bridges along its main length. That is because much of the region is remote and inaccessible by road. Transportation is done by boat or plane, and building bridges is often impossible due to flooding and terrain.

Iceland Has No Forests

Iceland was once covered in trees, but early settlers cut them down for farming and fuel. Harsh winds and volcanic soil prevented most of them from growing back. Today, reforestation efforts are underway, but Iceland remains one of the most treeless countries in the world.

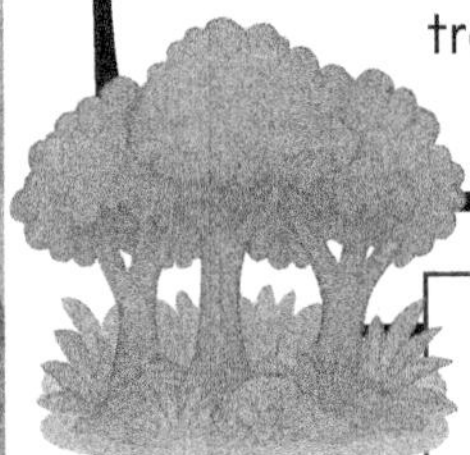

Japan Has Earthquake Alarms

Japan uses one of the fastest earthquake warning systems on Earth. Sensors detect waves underground and send alerts to phones, TVs, and trains seconds before shaking begins. This short window helps people take cover, stop machinery, and avoid injuries in high-risk areas.

Russia Has Eleven Time Zones

Russia is so vast that it stretches across eleven time zones. When people in the far east are going to bed, others in the west are just starting their day. To keep things simple for government work, some institutions use a standard time across the whole country.

Indonesia Has Many Islands

Indonesia is the largest island nation in the world, made up of more than seventeen thousand islands. Many are uninhabited, and some still have unexplored ecosystems. With hundreds of languages and cultures, it is one of the most diverse places on Earth.

The Sahara Was Once Green

Thousands of years ago, the Sahara Desert was a lush grassland with lakes and animals. Evidence shows that hippos and crocodiles once lived there. Climate shifts turned the region into the desert we know today. Scientists believe it may become green again in the distant future.

Australia Has Pink Lakes

In parts of Australia, you can find lakes that are bubblegum pink. The color comes from algae and bacteria that produce pigments in salty water. Lake Hillier is one of the most famous examples, and the color stays bright even when the water is removed.

Egypt Is Mostly Empty

Over 90 percent of Egypt's population lives along the Nile River, even though the country is massive. The rest of the land is mostly desert. This makes Egypt one of the most unevenly populated countries in the world, with entire cities built along a narrow green strip.

China Borders Fourteen Countries

China shares its borders with more countries than almost any other nation on Earth. Fourteen nations touch its boundaries, including India, Russia, and Vietnam. This makes China one of the most geopolitically complex countries in terms of trade, culture, and diplomacy.

There Is A City With No Roads

In Venice, Italy, there are almost no cars or roads. People get around using boats, walking paths, and narrow canals. The entire city is built on wooden piles sunk into muddy ground. It is a living example of how architecture can adapt to water instead of fighting it.

Antarctica Has No Permanent Residents

Antarctica is the only continent without cities or permanent population. Scientists live there temporarily at research stations, but no one is born or grows up there. It is the coldest, driest, and windiest place on Earth—and also one of the most peaceful, protected by international agreement.

Some Borders Are Straight Lines

In parts of Africa and North America, country borders are straight lines with no relation to natural geography. Many of these were drawn during colonial times with rulers on maps, not with knowledge of the land. This has caused conflicts and confusion that still affect politics today.

Greenland Is Mostly Ice

Despite its name, Greenland is covered by ice, while nearby Iceland is much greener. The naming may have been a marketing trick by early explorers hoping to attract settlers. Greenland's ice sheet is so thick that if it melted completely, it would raise sea levels by several meters.

Brazil Has A Hidden Desert

In northeastern Brazil lies Lençóis Maranhenses, a rare desert made of white sand dunes that fill with freshwater during the rainy season. The result is a surreal mix of desert and crystal-clear lagoons. It looks like a computer animation, but it is completely real and naturally formed.

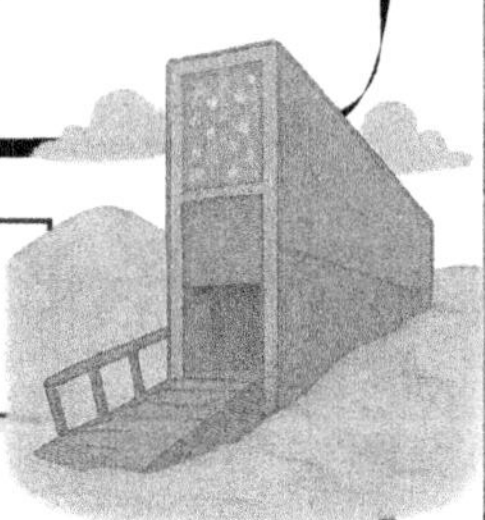

Norway Has A Seed Vault

Deep inside a mountain in the Arctic, Norway stores backup seeds from almost every major crop in the world. The Svalbard Global Seed Vault was built to protect biodiversity in case of global disasters. It is one of the safest and coldest storage facilities on Earth.

India Has A Living Bridge

In the forests of Meghalaya, people use the roots of rubber trees to grow living bridges. These root bridges are guided across rivers and can take decades to form. Once mature, they are strong enough to carry people and last for centuries without concrete or metal.

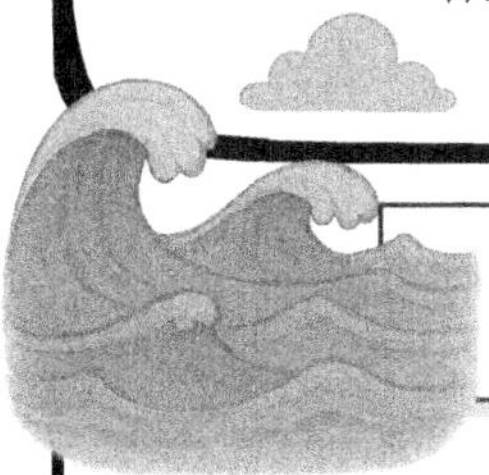

There Is A Sea Without Shores

The Sargasso Sea is a region in the Atlantic Ocean that has no land borders. Instead, it is defined by ocean currents. It is filled with floating seaweed and serves as a nursery for sea turtles and eels. Unlike other seas, it exists only because of water movement, not geography.

Finland Has Thousands Of Saunas

With a population of around five million, Finland has more than three million saunas. They are found in homes, offices, and even some buses. Saunas are considered essential to Finnish culture, and it is common for people to sit in silence together as a form of relaxation and bonding.

Ethiopia Uses A Different Calendar

Ethiopia follows a calendar that is about seven years behind the one used in most of the world. It has thirteen months and celebrates New Year in September. The country also uses a different time system where the day starts at sunrise, not midnight.

Chile Is Extremely Long And Thin

Chile stretches over four thousand kilometers from north to south but is rarely more than two hundred kilometers wide. This unique shape gives it a huge variety of climates, from the world's driest desert in the north to glaciers and forests in the south.

Some Countries Have Two Capitals

A few countries, like South Africa, use more than one city as a capital. South Africa has a legislative capital, an executive capital, and a judicial capital in three different places. This setup helps spread power and balance regional interests within the country.

Monaco Is Smaller Than A Park

Monaco is one of the smallest countries in the world. It is smaller than Central Park in New York City and can be walked across in under an hour. Despite its size, it has its own royal family, international borders, and a famously high population density.

Bangladesh Has Floating Schools

In regions where seasonal floods shut down roads and buildings, Bangladesh has created floating schools, libraries, and clinics. These solar-powered boats travel to remote villages and allow education and health care to continue even during heavy monsoon rains.

The Danube Crosses Ten Countries

The Danube River flows through more countries than any other river on Earth. It crosses ten nations in Europe and connects cities, cultures, and economies along its path. It has been a vital trade route since ancient times and remains central to European geography.

Lake Baikal Is The Deepest

Lake Baikal in Siberia is the deepest freshwater lake in the world. It reaches over 1,600 meters and contains more water than all the Great Lakes of North America combined. It is also one of the oldest lakes and home to unique species found nowhere else.

The Alps Keep Growing

The Alps were formed by the collision of the African and European tectonic plates, and they are still rising slowly each year. Erosion wears them down at the same time, but geologists have measured a net upward movement, meaning the famous mountain range is still changing.

Vatican City Has Its Own Army

Vatican City, the smallest country in the world, has its own security force called the Swiss Guard. These soldiers wear Renaissance-style uniforms but are trained professionals who protect the Pope and the city. They must be Swiss citizens and have military training before applying.

The Philippines Have Over 100 Languages

The Philippines are home to more than 180 spoken languages. Filipino and English are official languages, but many people also speak regional ones like Cebuano, Ilocano, or Waray. Language diversity reflects the country's island geography and rich cultural heritage.

The Dead Sea Lets You Float

The Dead Sea, located between Jordan and Israel, has such a high salt concentration that people can float effortlessly on its surface. It is almost ten times saltier than the ocean, which makes it nearly impossible for fish or plants to survive. That is why it is called "dead."

New Zealand Has No Snakes

There are no native snake species in New Zealand. The country has strict biosecurity laws to keep it that way. While nearby Australia is famous for its snakes, New Zealand remains snake-free, which makes it unique among large island nations.

Some Islands Are Disappearing

Rising sea levels are causing small island nations like Tuvalu and the Maldives to shrink. Some may disappear completely within decades. These countries are raising awareness and calling for global action, since their cultures and homes are directly threatened by climate change.

The Nile Is Disputed

The Nile River flows through eleven countries and is the longest river in the world. Its water is a source of political tension because several countries depend on it for survival. Dams and usage rights are ongoing points of negotiation in the region.

Green Walls Fight Heat

In cities around the world, vertical gardens are being added to buildings to reduce heat and clean the air. These green walls help lower temperatures, save energy, and make concrete landscapes more livable. They are part of a growing movement toward sustainable urban design.

The Universe

Saturn Could Float On Water

If you could find a bathtub big enough, Saturn would float. That is because it is made mostly of gas and is far less dense than Earth. Of course, a bathtub that size does not exist, but the idea shows just how strange the planets in our solar system really are.

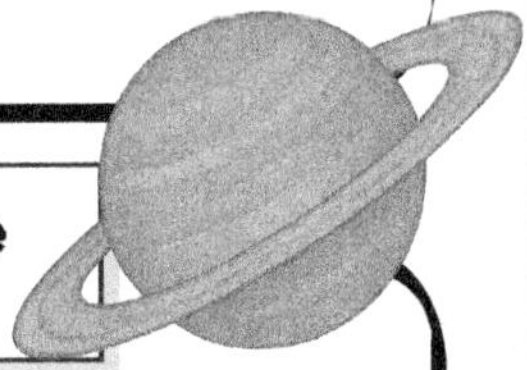

Neutron Stars Are Ultra Dense

A neutron star forms when a massive star collapses. Its matter is packed so tightly that a single teaspoon of it would weigh several billion tons. These stars are only about twenty kilometers wide but have more mass than the entire sun.

The Moon Moves Away Slowly

The Moon is drifting away from Earth by about four centimeters every year. This happens because of gravitational forces between Earth and the Moon. In the distant future, this will change how eclipses look and may even affect Earth's rotation.

The Sun Is Loud

If space could carry sound, the sun would be louder than a rock concert. Scientists estimate it produces noise at around 100 decibels on the surface and even louder deeper inside. Luckily, space is a vacuum, so we do not hear a thing. Earth is peaceful but the sun is basically screaming.

Black Holes Warp Time

Near a black hole, gravity is so intense that time slows down. The closer you get, the more extreme the effect becomes. This is not science fiction, it has been confirmed through physics and observed in experiments. Time is not fixed but depends on gravity and motion.

There Are More Stars Than Grains Of Sand

Astronomers estimate that the observable universe contains more stars than there are grains of sand on all the beaches on Earth. Each star may have its own planets, moons, and even life. The scale of the universe is almost impossible to imagine.

Jupiter Has A Giant Storm

Jupiter's Great Red Spot is a massive storm that has been raging for at least 350 years. It is so large that Earth could fit inside it. The storm spins counterclockwise and changes size over time, but it still shows no sign of stopping.

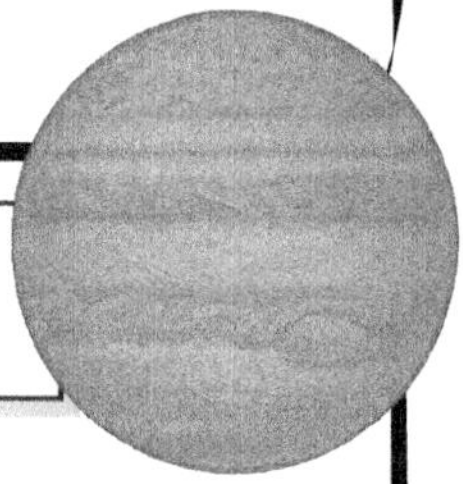

Light Takes Time To Travel

When you look at stars, you are seeing them as they were in the past. Light from the sun takes about eight minutes to reach Earth. Light from distant galaxies can take millions or even billions of years. So in a way, telescopes are also time machines.

Space Smells Like Burnt Steak

Astronauts have reported that their suits smell like seared meat after a spacewalk. The scent comes from high-energy particles clinging to their gear. Since you cannot actually smell anything in space, the odor appears once they return to the ship. It is one of the strangest side effects of floating around Earth.

You Can See The Past

Some galaxies are so far away that their light has taken billions of years to reach us. When we observe them, we see them as they looked when Earth had no animals, no plants, and no continents. Looking deeper into space means looking further into the past.

The Universe Has No Center

The universe is expanding in all directions, but it does not have a single center point. Every galaxy sees others moving away. This means the universe has no edge and no middle. It is not expanding into something, it is space itself that is growing.

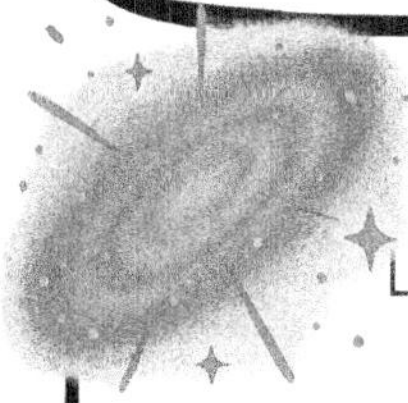

Time Began With The Big Bang

According to current physics, time itself began when the universe was born. Before the Big Bang, there was no time, no space, and no matter. This idea is based on Einstein's theories and supported by observations of cosmic background radiation.

There Is A Coldest Place

In space, temperatures can get close to absolute zero, where all atomic motion stops. The coldest known natural spot in the universe is the Boomerang Nebula. It is even colder than the background temperature of space itself, due to rapid gas expansion.

Some Planets Rain Metal

On the exoplanet WASP-76b, the atmosphere is so hot that metals like iron evaporate. On the cooler side of the planet, the vapor condenses and falls as liquid metal rain. Other planets have glass storms, acid clouds, or winds thousands of kilometers per hour.

Dark Matter Shapes The Universe

Most of the matter in the universe is invisible. Dark matter does not emit or absorb light, but its gravity affects how galaxies move. Without it, galaxies would fly apart. Scientists still do not know what it is made of, but it holds the universe together.

Some Stars Pulse Like Hearts

Certain stars called variable stars expand and contract in regular cycles. These pulses can change their brightness dramatically. Astronomers use these patterns to measure distances in space because their rhythm is predictable, like a cosmic heartbeat.

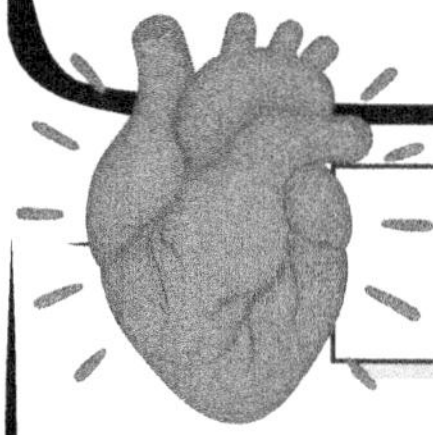

The Moon Has Moonquakes

The Moon is not as still as it looks. It experiences quakes caused by tidal forces, meteorite impacts, and thermal expansion. Some of these moonquakes are strong enough to crack the lunar surface. Unlike Earthquakes, they can last for hours due to the Moon's dry structure.

The Universe Is Still Expanding

The universe has been expanding since the Big Bang, and it is speeding up, not slowing down. This unexpected acceleration is linked to a mysterious force called dark energy. No one knows what dark energy is, but it makes up most of the universe's energy content.

Mars Has The Tallest Volcano

Olympus Mons on Mars is the tallest volcano in the solar system. It rises about 22 kilometers high, nearly three times the height of Mount Everest. Because Mars has weaker gravity and no tectonic plate movement, the volcano could grow much larger than anything on Earth.

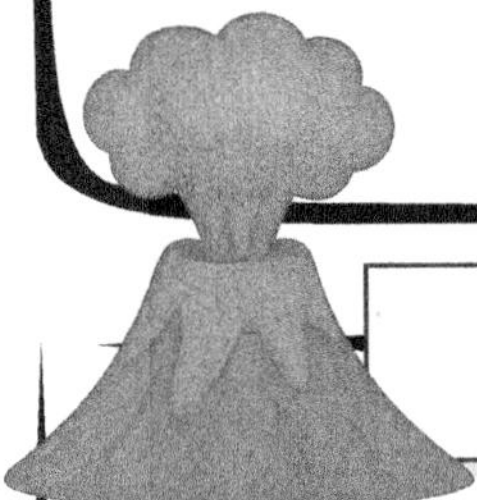

One Day May Last Forever

On some planets, the length of a day changes drastically over time. If a planet becomes tidally locked, one side always faces its star. That means one side has eternal daylight while the other is in permanent night. Mercury is close to this and rotates very slowly.

Light Can Be Bent

Massive objects like galaxies and black holes bend light as it passes by. This effect, called gravitational lensing, lets scientists see galaxies that would otherwise be hidden. It also confirms that space itself is not a flat surface but can be warped by gravity.

Most Stars Die Quietly

While some stars end in violent explosions called supernovae, most fade out quietly. Smaller stars like our sun shed their outer layers and become white dwarfs. These remnants glow softly for billions of years before going dark completely. The universe is full of quiet endings.

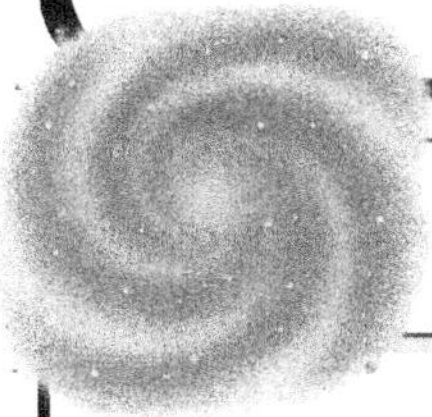

Galaxies Spin Like Pinwheels

Most galaxies, including the Milky Way, rotate around a central point. Their spiral arms are made of billions of stars orbiting a dense core. This spin keeps them stable and gives them their iconic shape. The exact reason for the structure is still not fully understood.

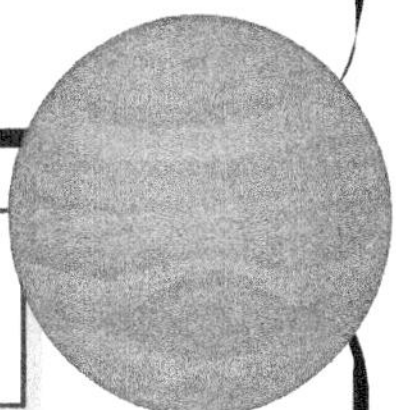

Venus Spins The Wrong Way

Venus rotates in the opposite direction to most planets. On Venus, the sun rises in the west and sets in the east. It also spins extremely slowly, making a single day on Venus longer than its entire year. Scientists believe a massive collision may have reversed its rotation.

The Milky Way Is Moving

Our entire galaxy is racing through space at about two million kilometers per hour. It is pulled by the gravity of other galaxies and clusters. Even though we do not feel it, Earth, the sun, and every star around us are on a cosmic journey.

Space Has A Background Glow

After the Big Bang, a faint glow of radiation remained behind. This cosmic microwave background fills the entire universe and provides a snapshot of what space looked like nearly fourteen billion years ago. It is one of the strongest pieces of evidence for how the universe began.

Some Stars Are Born In Pairs

Many stars form in binary systems, where two stars orbit a shared center. Some even steal matter from each other or collide in spectacular bursts. Binary systems are common and help astronomers understand how stars evolve, merge, or explode.

The Universe Has A Sound

While space is a vacuum, scientists have converted cosmic data into sound. Using wave frequencies from stars and gas clouds, researchers have created audio versions of what the universe would "sound" like if we could hear it. The result is a deep, eerie hum unlike anything on Earth.

There Are Rogue Planets

Not all planets orbit stars. Some wander through space alone, without a sun. These rogue planets were likely ejected from their systems during formation. They drift in darkness, possibly with underground heat sources or even oceans beneath icy crusts.

Stars Come In Many Colors

Stars are not all white or yellow. They come in colors based on their temperature. Blue stars are the hottest, followed by white, yellow, orange, and red as the coolest. Our sun is a yellow dwarf, balanced in the middle of the stellar temperature range.

Space Travel Alters The Body

Astronauts experience physical changes in space, including bone loss, muscle weakening, and fluid shifts. Without gravity, body systems adapt in unusual ways. Some astronauts return taller due to spinal expansion, though the effect is temporary. Studying these changes helps scientists understand how humans might survive long-term missions.

Mars Has Seasons Like Earth

Mars tilts on its axis, just like Earth, which creates seasons. However, because its orbit is more elliptical, the seasons are not evenly spaced. Martian winters can be harsh, and summer is short but intense. Dust storms and thin air make the climate even more extreme.

You Could Fit A Million Earths Into The Sun

The sun is so large that about one million Earths could fit inside it. Despite this, it is considered a medium-sized star. Larger stars exist that could contain multiple suns and still have room left over. Scale in space is often beyond human imagination.

Galaxies Collide Over Time

Galaxies are not fixed in place. They move through space and sometimes crash into each other. In about four billion years, the Milky Way and the Andromeda galaxy will merge. Stars are so far apart that few will collide directly, but the shape of both galaxies will change forever.

The Sun Will Expand

In about five billion years, the sun will run out of fuel and expand into a red giant. It will swallow Mercury and Venus and possibly Earth. After that, it will shrink into a white dwarf and slowly fade. Stars are not eternal, even though they burn for billions of years.

Saturn's Rings Are Temporary

Saturn's famous rings are made of ice and rock, but they are slowly disappearing. Gravity and solar radiation are pulling the material into the planet. Scientists believe the rings will vanish completely within the next 100 million years. In cosmic terms, they are just a phase.

History

Cleopatra Lived Surprisingly Recent

Cleopatra ruled Egypt around 30 BCE. By then, the Great Pyramid of Giza was already over 2,500 years old. That means Cleopatra is closer in time to space travel and smartphones than to the building of the pyramids she famously ruled beside.

Ancient Romans Had Takeout

Archaeologists have discovered ancient Roman "fast food" restaurants called thermopolia. These places served hot meals to people who did not cook at home. Painted menus and built-in serving pots show that quick, affordable food was popular in cities like Pompeii nearly two thousand years ago.

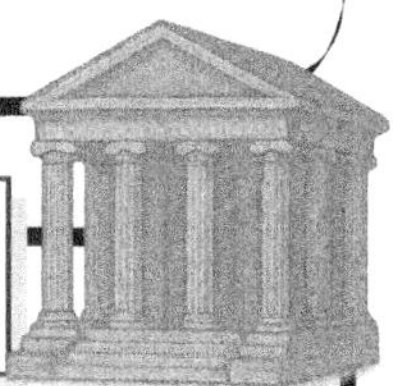

A War Lasted Only 38 Minutes

The shortest recorded war in history happened in 1896 between Britain and the Sultanate of Zanzibar. After a dispute over succession, British forces opened fire. The conflict ended in just 38 minutes. The sultan's palace was destroyed and a new leader was installed almost immediately.

Napoleon Was Not Short

Napoleon Bonaparte is often remembered as being unusually short, but he was actually of average height for his time. Confusion arose because French and British measurements were different. British propaganda exaggerated his size to make him seem less threatening.

The Eiffel Tower Was Hated

When the Eiffel Tower was built in 1889, many Parisians thought it was hideous. Artists and writers called it a metal monster. Today it is one of the most recognized landmarks in the world. What started as a temporary structure became a symbol of the entire country.

Vikings Reached America First

Around the year 1000, Norse explorer Leif Erikson landed on the coast of what is now Canada. He called the place Vinland and built a small settlement. This happened almost 500 years before Columbus crossed the Atlantic. The site, L'Anse aux Meadows, is now a UNESCO World Heritage location.

Shakespeare Invented Over 1,000 Words

William Shakespeare coined or popularized many English words and phrases still used today. Examples include lonely, excitement, eyeball, and break the ice. His creative use of language helped shape modern English, even for people who have never read his plays.

The Great Fire Helped Stop The Plague

In 1666, a massive fire swept through London, destroying much of the city. As terrible as it was, it also helped wipe out the rats and fleas that spread the bubonic plague. The fire unintentionally ended one of the deadliest outbreaks in European history.

The Berlin Wall Divided Families

Built in 1961, the Berlin Wall split East and West Berlin overnight. Families, friends, and couples were suddenly cut off with no warning. Some people jumped from windows or tunneled underground to escape. The wall stood for 28 years and became a symbol of the Cold War.

The First Computer Was Ancient

The Antikythera mechanism, found in a Greek shipwreck, dates back over 2,000 years. It used gears to predict eclipses and track celestial events. Experts call it the world's first analog computer. Its complexity was not matched for over a thousand years.

China Built A Giant Fleet

In the 1400s, Admiral Zheng He led massive Chinese voyages across the Indian Ocean. His ships were so large they made European vessels look tiny. These expeditions reached Africa, Arabia, and Southeast Asia but were eventually stopped as China turned inward.

Ancient Persians Used Refrigeration

Over 2,000 years ago, Persians built underground structures called yakhchals to store ice and food in the desert. They used evaporative cooling and clever airflow systems to keep temperatures below freezing—even in summer. It was early climate control without electricity.

Julius Caesar Was Kidnapped

As a young man, Julius Caesar was captured by pirates. While held for ransom, he joked with them, demanded they raise the ransom, and promised to come back and kill them. Once released, he did exactly that. It was an early sign of his ambition and ruthlessness.

Oxford Is Older Than Aztec Empire

The University of Oxford was teaching students as early as 1096. That is hundreds of years before the Aztec Empire rose in what is now Mexico. While Oxford grew quietly in England, the Aztecs were still centuries away from building their famous pyramids.

Troy Was A Real City

Long thought to be only myth, the city of Troy was discovered in the 1800s in modern-day Turkey. Archaeologists found ruins matching Homer's description. While the Trojan Horse story remains legend, the war itself may have been based on real events.

A Polish Bear Fought In War

During World War II, Polish soldiers adopted a bear named Wojtek who carried ammunition during battles in Italy. He drank beer, smoked cigarettes, and marched with the troops. After the war, he retired in a zoo and became a national legend.

Napoleon's Rabbit Disaster

In 1807, Napoleon arranged a rabbit hunt for his officers. Hundreds of tame rabbits were released, but instead of running, they charged him. The emperor and his men were overwhelmed and forced to flee the field. The animals had been fed by humans before and thought Napoleon was bringing lunch.

Emperor Nero Had A Rotating Ceiling

In ancient Rome, Emperor Nero built a palace with a dining room that had a rotating ceiling. It mimicked the stars and sprinkled rose petals and perfume over guests during meals. The mechanism was powered by hidden slaves and showed off his obsession with luxury and spectacle.

A Dancing Plague Broke Out

In 1518, dozens of people in Strasbourg suddenly began dancing uncontrollably in the streets. Some danced for days without stopping, and a few reportedly collapsed and died. Historians still debate the cause, with theories ranging from mass hysteria to contaminated bread.

Ancient Toilets Had No Privacy

In ancient Rome, public toilets were long stone benches with holes, used side by side without dividers. People sat together, chatting while doing their business. Some places even had shared sponge sticks for wiping, which were rinsed and reused between users.

Romans Washed With Urine

In ancient Rome, laundries cleaned clothes using human urine. It was collected from public jars and prized for its ammonia, which broke down stains. Workers stomped the clothes in large vats of it. The emperor even taxed urine collection, making it a source of both hygiene and income.

Finland Switched Sides

During World War II, Finland first fought against the Soviet Union with help from Nazi Germany. But in 1944, they turned on Germany and drove out German troops. Finland is one of the only countries to have officially fought on both sides during the same war and still stayed independent.

A Pope Tried A Corpse

In 897, Pope Stephen VI held a bizarre trial for his dead predecessor, Pope Formosus. The body was exhumed, dressed in robes, and placed on a throne. Found guilty, it was thrown into the river. The event chocked the public and became known as the Cadaver Synod.

Eiffel's Secret Apartment

Gustave Eiffel secretly built a small private apartment at the top of the Eiffel Tower. He used it to host scientists and important guests. Unlike the rest of the tower, it was cozy and elegant. Today, the room is preserved and can be seen through a glass window.

Japan Measured Time With Smell

In 10th-century Japan, people used incense clocks that released different scents each hour. Nobles could tell time by recognizing the changing smell. These devices blended timekeeping with art, turning daily schedules into something quiet and poetic.

New Zealand Let Women Vote First

In 1893, New Zealand became the first country in the world to give women the right to vote in national elections. The change came after years of activism led by women like Kate Sheppard. It marked the beginning of a global shift toward voting equality.

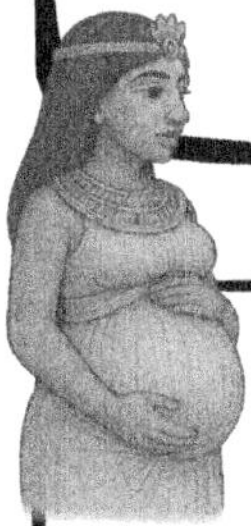

Ancient Egypt Had Pregnancy Tests

Egyptian texts from 3,500 years ago describe pregnancy tests using wheat and barley. A woman would urinate on seeds for several days. If they sprouted, she was considered pregnant. Modern tests have shown this method can sometimes work due to hormonal changes in urine.

London Once Had Ice Fairs

In the 1600s and 1700s, the River Thames would freeze so solid in winter that people held entire festivals on the ice. Booths, bonfires, and even ice bowling took place. These "Frost Fairs" ended after the river's flow changed and winters grew milder.

Ancient Chinese Used Paper Armor

Some Chinese soldiers wore armor made of layered paper. It was surprisingly effective against arrows and could be repaired easily. The paper was soaked in water or vinegar to resist fire and became a cheap but clever defense material during certain periods.

Medieval Animals Were Put On Trial

In parts of medieval Europe, animals could be put on trial for crimes. Pigs, rats, and even insects were charged with offenses like theft or murder. They had lawyers, court dates, and were sometimes sentenced to death. These trials reflected religious beliefs of the time.

The Great Emu War Failed

In 1932, Australia sent soldiers with machine guns to control a group of emus damaging farmland. The birds outran the soldiers and scattered quickly. Despite firing thousands of rounds, the military failed to stop them. The emus won, and the operation was quietly abandoned.

Ancient Greece Had Robots

Inventors in ancient Greece built early mechanical devices that acted like robots. Hero of Alexandria designed automatic doors, water-powered machines, and even a puppet theater. Though basic, these inventions show how far imagination and engineering reached more than 2,000 years ago.

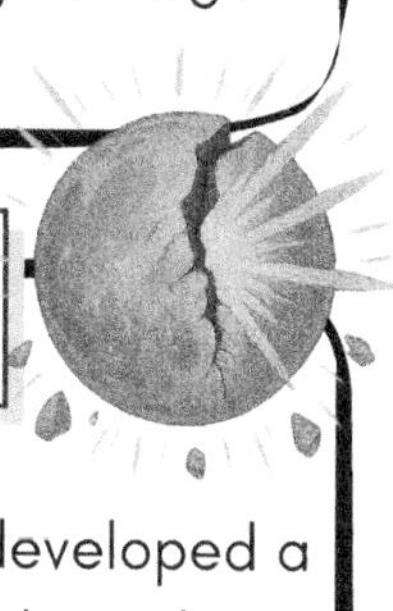

The US Once Planned A Moon Explosion

During the Cold War, the United States developed a secret plan to detonate a nuclear bomb on the Moon to show strength. The idea was to create a visible explosion that could be seen from Earth. Thankfully, the project was canceled before it left the ground.

The Colosseum Was Flooded

In ancient Rome, the Colosseum was sometimes flooded to stage mock naval battles. Real ships and actors reenacted sea warfare for public entertainment. The practice was eventually stopped, but it showed the extreme efforts the Romans made to impress a crowd.

Napoleon Changed Time In France

Napoleon introduced a new calendar during the French Revolution. It had ten-day weeks, renamed months, and decimal time. The idea was to break from religion and tradition, but people hated it. It lasted just 12 years before France returned to the old system.

A Town Elected A Dog As Mayor

In 1997, a small town in Kentucky elected a dog named Goofy as mayor. It was part of a fundraising event, but locals loved the idea and repeated it with other animals in future elections. These symbolic mayors helped promote community projects and bring national attention.

Sports &
Games

The Olympics Once Had Art

From 1912 to 1948, the Olympic Games included competitions in painting, literature, music, and architecture. Artists submitted works inspired by sport and were awarded medals. The events were removed because many participants were professionals, while athletes were supposed to be amateurs.

Chess Has Been Played For Centuries

Chess originated in India over 1,400 years ago and slowly evolved into the modern version we know today. Rules changed in the Middle Ages, and the queen became the most powerful piece. Some famous matches have lasted over 20 hours, with players losing weight during play.

Boxing Has Ancient Roots

Boxing dates back to Mesopotamia and Ancient Greece, where fighters used leather straps instead of gloves. It was a brutal sport with few rules. In ancient Rome, some matches ended in death. The modern version evolved in England, with standardized rules introduced in the 18th century.

eSports Fill Stadiums

Competitive video gaming, or eSports, now draws millions of viewers worldwide. Major tournaments fill stadiums and top players earn more than traditional athletes. Games like League of Legends and Fortnite have become global spectator sports with professional teams and coaches.

Tug Of War Was Olympic

Between 1900 and 1920, tug of war was an official Olympic sport. Teams of eight pulled on ropes in dramatic contests. It was eventually removed as the games narrowed focus, but efforts to bring it back as a modern event still appear from time to time.

The First Soccer Ball Was A Bladder

Early versions of football (soccer) used inflated animal bladders as balls. In medieval Europe, pig bladders were common. The modern round ball shape only became standard in the 20th century, after rubber and synthetic materials replaced animal parts.

Cricket Matches Can Last Days

Traditional Test cricket matches are played over five days and can still end in a draw. Players take breaks for tea, lunch, and sometimes bad weather. Fans bring books, picnics, and patience. Despite its slow pace, it remains one of the most beloved sports in countries like India and England.

The Oldest Team Sport Is Polo

Polo is one of the world's oldest team sports, dating back to ancient Persia over 2,000 years ago. Originally played by cavalry units to train for battle, it spread through Asia and later became popular with European nobility. Today it remains a symbol of prestige.

Wimbledon Still Uses Grass

Wimbledon is the only major tennis tournament still played on natural grass. The surface makes the game faster and less predictable. Groundskeepers monitor every blade, and matches can be delayed for light rain. Tradition is so strong that players must wear white.

Table Tennis Was An After-Dinner Game

Table tennis began as a Victorian parlor game, played on dining tables using books as nets and rounded corks as balls. It evolved into a serious sport, now played competitively worldwide. The fastest smashes reach speeds over 110 kilometers per hour.

Sumo Wrestlers Have Rankings

In Japan, sumo is not just a sport but a deeply traditional system with strict rankings. Wrestlers live in training stables and follow strict diets and rituals. Only the top division earns a salary, while lower-ranked fighters clean, cook, and serve their superiors.

Chess Boxing Is Real

Chess boxing combines brain and brawn. Competitors alternate between rounds of boxing and chess. A match can end by knockout or checkmate. The sport began as a performance idea but gained real followers. It requires both mental focus and physical toughness.

Olympic Gold Is Mostly Silver

Modern Olympic gold medals are made mostly of silver and coated in about six grams of gold. The last time medals were made of solid gold was in 1912. Despite the name, the value comes from the achievement, not the metal.

Football Fans Shook The Earth

During a 2011 game in Seattle, a touchdown celebration by fans caused a small earthquake. Seismic sensors registered the movement, which came to be called the “Beast Quake.” It showed how intense crowd energy can physically move the ground.

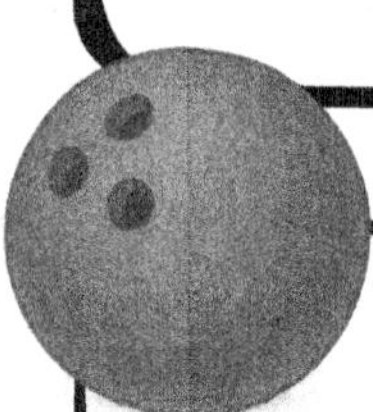

Bowling Was Banned In England

In the 14th century, King Edward III banned bowling because it distracted soldiers from practicing archery. The law was enforced for over 300 years. Today, bowling is purely recreational, but it was once considered a threat to national defense.

Boxing Gloves Made It Bloodier

Before gloves, boxers used bare fists and fought more cautiously. When padded gloves were introduced, fighters hit harder with less risk to their hands. Ironically, this led to more head injuries and knockouts, making the sport more brutal in some ways.

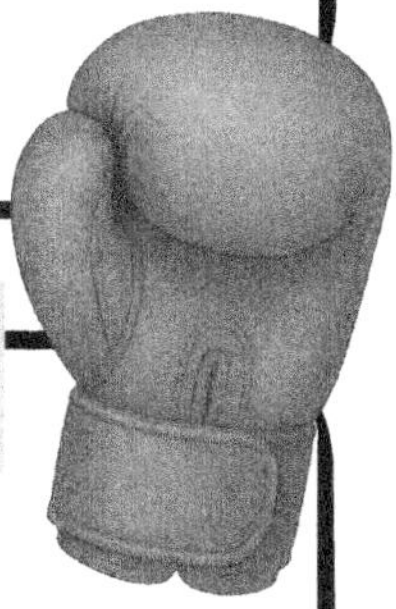

Olympic Medals Were Once Paintings

In the early 20th century, athletes were awarded medals not just for sports, but also for painting, sculpture, and music. The artworks had to be inspired by sport. Some competitors even won medals in both athletic and artistic categories.

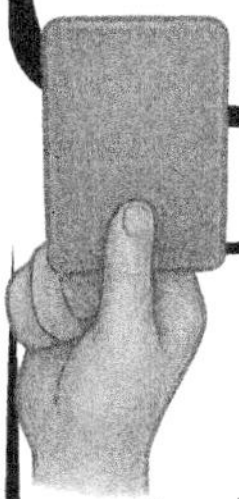

A Referee Once Got A Red Card

At the 1974 World Cup, a referee accidentally dropped his red card. A player picked it up and jokingly showed it to the referee, who then gave the player an actual red card for mocking authority. It was one of the strangest expulsions in football history.

Olympic Athletes Used To Compete Naked

In ancient Greece, Olympic athletes competed completely naked. It was seen as a tribute to the gods and a celebration of the human body. The word "gymnasium" even comes from the Greek word for naked, and athletes often oiled themselves before events.

Snowboarding Was Once Banned

When snowboarding first appeared in the 1980s, many ski resorts refused to allow it. It was considered dangerous, rebellious, and disrespectful to tradition. Over time, it gained popularity, became an Olympic sport in 1998, and helped reinvent winter sports culture.

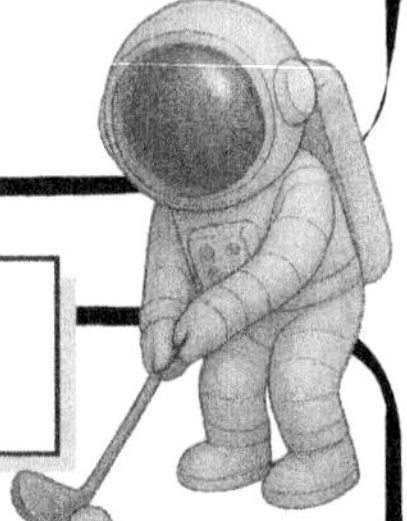

Golf Was Played On The Moon

In 1971, astronaut Alan Shepard hit two golf balls on the Moon using a modified club. With low gravity and no atmosphere, the ball flew far, though no one knows exactly how far. It was a lighthearted moment during the Apollo 14 mission.

Early Ice Skates Used Bones

Long before metal blades, people in northern Europe tied animal bones to their feet to glide across frozen lakes. The bones were often sharpened and worn with leather straps. Skating evolved from a survival skill into a global winter pastime.

Formula 1 Drivers Lose Weight

During a single race, Formula 1 drivers can lose up to three kilograms from sweat and strain. Cockpit temperatures often exceed 50°C, and the G-forces require intense physical strength. Despite sitting down, F1 is one of the most physically demanding sports.

Skiing Was A Form Of Transport

Long before it became a sport, skiing was used as a way to hunt, travel, and survive winter in Scandinavia. Cave paintings over 5,000 years old show people on skis. The first recorded ski race took place in Norway in the 18th century.

Parkour Started As Military Training

Parkour, the sport of moving efficiently through obstacles, was developed in France by military instructors. It evolved from training methods used to build endurance, agility, and survival skills. Today it's a global street sport focused on creativity and flow.

Olympic Torches Went Underwater

For the 2000 Olympics in Sydney, the torch relay included an underwater leg. A diver carried a specially designed torch through part of the Great Barrier Reef. It used a chemical reaction to keep burning underwater, making it one of the most dramatic torch moments ever.

Ice Hockey Was Played With Cow Dung

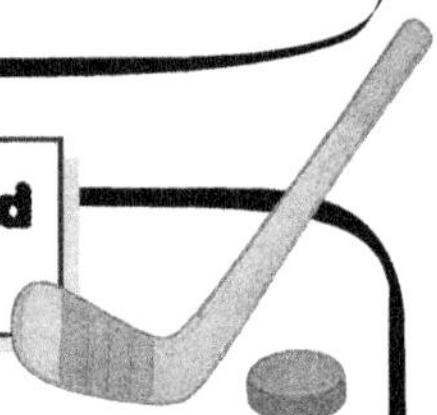

Before standardized pucks, early ice hockey players used frozen cow dung as a puck. It was flat, cheap, and easy to slide across ice. Thankfully, rubber pucks were introduced in the 1870s, ending one of the sport's least hygienic traditions.

Thanks For Pooping With Us!

If you made it this far, you've officially leveled up in useless knowledge. Congrats!

We hope this book made you laugh, raise an eyebrow, or shout "Wait, what?!" at least once. If it did, our job here is done.

Got feedback, fun fact suggestions, or a weird story of your own? We'd love to hear from you. Reach out at:
contact@bergmann-publishing.com

Now go forth and casually drop facts into conversations like the trivia ninja you've become.

And hey, don't forget to wash your hands.

Publication Information
Author: Willy Wiper
Address: 105 Albert Palace Mansions
Lurline Gardens
London SW11 4DH
United Kingdom

Printed in Dunstable, United Kingdom

78661472R00070